3 7 99

D0203915

PERSPECTIVES
ON
LEADERSHIP

PERSPECTIVES ON LEADERSHIP

From the Science of Management to Its Spiritual Heart

Gilbert W. Fairholm

QUORUM BOOKS
Westport, Connecticut • London

Library of Congress Cataloging-in-Publication Data

Fairholm, Gilbert W.
  Perspectives on leadership : from the science of management to its
spiritual heart / Gilbert W. Fairholm.
    p. cm.
  Includes bibliographical references and index.
  ISBN 1–56720–202–0 (alk. paper)
  1. Leadership—Moral and ethical aspects. 2. Leadership—
Religious aspects. 3. Management—Moral and ethical aspects.
4. Management—Religious aspects. I. Title.
HD57.7.F352 1998
658.4'092—dc21   97–48615

British Library Cataloguing in Publication Data is available.

Library of Congress Catalog Card Number: 97–48615
ISBN: 1–56720–202–0

First published in 1998

Quorum Books, 88 Post Road West, Westport, CT 06881
An imprint of Greenwood Publishing Group, Inc.

Printed in the United States of America

The paper used in this book complies with the
Permanent Paper Standard issued by the National
Information Standards Organization (Z39.48–1984).

10 9 8 7 6 5 4 3 2 1

Contents

Preface   ix

Introduction   xiii

The Leadership Mind-Set / Alternative Ways to Think about Leadership / Levels of Leadership / Summary

Part I   **Leadership as Management**   **1**

1   Evolution of the Manager as Leader   3

Scientific Management / Behavioral Science Approaches / Systems Management and Quantitative Management / Organizational Structure and Management

2   Purposes of Management   17

Modern Functions of Management

Part II   **Leadership Excellence**   **23**

3   Leadership as Excellent Management   25

Historical Threads of the Quest for Quality / The Modern Quality Focus / Principles of Leadership Excellence

4   Defining Quality Operationally   31

*Doing Quality Work / Deming's Management
Philosophy / Juran's Quality Philosophy*

5   Skills Needed for Leadership Excellence   39

*Personal Leader Action Technologies / Leader
Action Technologies Directed toward
Stakeholders / Leader Actions to Change the
Organizational Surround / Summary and
Conclusions*

Part III   Values Leadership   47

6   Overview of Past Leadership Theories   49

*Theories of Who the Leader IS / Theories of What
the Leader DOES / Theories of Where Leadership
TAKES PLACE / Shortcomings of Current
Models*

7   Defining Values-based Leadership   55

*The Values-based Leadership Philosophy / The
Role of Leadership / Review of New Values-based
Leadership Theories / The Values Theory Basis
for Leadership*

8   Principles of Values-based Leadership Theory   61

Core Principles of Values-based Leadership

9   The Values-based Leadership Model   67

*Elements of Values-based Leadership / Results of
the Values-based Leadership Philosophy /
Summary*

Part IV   Trust Leadership   73

10   Unified Cultures   75

*The Impact of Culture on Leadership / The
Impact of Trust on Culture and on Leadership /
Integrating Values in Culture*

11   Defining Culture   81

Elements of Definition

12   Shaping Culture   87

Techniques for Shaping Culture

13 The Leadership of Trust 91

The Trust-Truth Model / Developing Trust / Leadership of the Trust Culture / Results of Trust Leadership

14 Leadership and Multiculturalism 103

Sameness amid Diversity / Leading a Culturally Diverse Work Force / Leading for Cultural Unity, Not Diversity / Obstacles to Shaping Trust Cultures

Part V The Spiritural Heart of Leadership 109

15 The Place of Spirit in Our Work Lives 111

Spirituality and Work / The Need for Spiritual Leadership

16 Defining Spiritual Leadership 117

Foundations of Spiritual Leadership / Definitional Elements of Spiritual Leadership

17 Problems with the Current Situation 123

Problems Encountered in Legitimatizing Spirit in Leadership / Pressures That Focus Our Spiritual Self at Work / The Power of Spirit

18 Understanding Spiritual Leadership at Work 129

The Force of Spirit / An Old/New Definition of Success / Practical (Work) Spirituality / Spiritual Leadership at Work / Integration of Spirituality into Secular Work Groups

19 Application of Spiritual Leadership at Work 137

Elements of Spiritual Leadership / The Spiritual Leadership Model

20 Applying Spiritual Leadership 143

Setting a Higher Moral Standard / Stewardship / Building Community / Other Spiritual Leadership Techniques

Bibliography 155

Index 163

Preface

Leading others is not easy. Senge says the leader bears an almost sacred duty to create conditions that enable people to grow and have happy and productive lives (Senge, 1990). The new leadership ideas put forward in the last 10–15 years begin to define this kind of leadership dealing with followers' core values. Yet, most established authors and some practitioners are locked into traditional thinking and have largely ignored these ideas. Nevertheless, the real leaders among us think in these terms and practice this kind of leadership, and they have done so for generations.

The problem is that theorists and practitioners have developed a mind-set that defines one kind of "leadership truth" and excludes any other alternatives. Any ideas about leadership that differ from this mind-set are generally rejected out of hand. Indeed, we do not easily move out of one reality into another. What we now believe to be true, given our particular experience, often seems to be the only truth. Some outside force must trigger reevaluating and rethinking. That triggering force to intellectual growth may be a new idea, a new situation, a new value, a new boss or some other significant emotional event—like a new book.

In the meantime, while theory tries to catch up with practice, leaders lead, writers write and trainers train, and the real basis of leadership continues to elude us. Certainly past leadership models have identified some critical elements of the leader's task. None fully describes current leader practice or guides beginning leaders in understanding and executing this role.

Leadership is an idea in motion. Our understanding of this most basic and widespread organizational relationship has been recast several times over the 100 years of modern management. Analysis of this stream of ideas points up several core ideas around which researchers and writers have developed elaborate structures to define and describe the leadership environment.

Thus, for much of this century, leadership has meant the technology of management. In this view leaders are those at the head of the firm, in authority and responsible for accomplishing its work. Some reserve the idea of leadership to mean only good management: the superlative qualities and actions of a few excellent organization heads. A few writers define leadership in change terms: meaning the task of instituting meaningful change and, more recently, the job of reconstructing the nature and character of the corporation and its workers.

Which of these models, if any, is the correct one to delineate the leadership process and environment is unclear. Some recent work adds ideas to the mix that begin to explore the impact on leading others on the basis of the leaders' and followers' innate values. Our core values define us and determine the goals we seek and the methods we will use to attain them. This research and our observation of literally thousands of leaders in our collective experience suggest that *everybody has values, and these values trigger our behavior*! Leadership takes place in a situation pregnant with values.

The power of our values in shaping our individual and collective lives is obvious. We all respond to the force of our deeply held values. Unfortunately, this truth did not find its way into past leadership models. But, given the importance of leadership in today's world, we cannot ignore this powerful way to think about the leadership process. Following this line of thinking holds promise of helping us understand more fully the leader-follower relationship and the environment in which it takes place. But, to make it work for us asks us to open our minds to new ways to think about, practice and measure leadership action.

Leadership is not merely insuring that rules and procedures are carried out efficiently. Surely it includes this productivity element. But it is more than that. It also deals with people in relationships. This view opens tremendous possibilities for personal growth and for being a positive influence in helping group members and those in the larger society change their lives for the better. For the purpose of leadership is to change lives!

By their actions, through the programs they manage and their personal behavior, leaders act to create a culture of individual progress and growth. Only in this activity is leadership enduring. It changes people, allows them to be different, better, than they were before our leadership. This is the essence of leadership—helping others to develop and mature and in the process maturing ourselves.

The leader is a servant first and then a boss. Many of the problems we have as leaders result because we tend to reverse this order of things. That is, we concentrate overmuch on bossing our followers—making them do what we want—instead of serving them by helping them be the best they can be in their jobs and otherwise. True leadership and service cannot be separated (Greenleaf, 1977). This is the message of leadership through the ages. The great leaders have always served their followers first and then led them into a new, better, more productive life.

Introduction

What makes a leader? What is leadership? What do leaders do? After 100 years of modern study, these remain cogent questions. Many writers have offered either general or specific answers over the years, but the discussion continues unabated. We have not yet resolved these questions to the satisfaction of most, and the search for acceptable answers continues.

Understanding the role and function of leadership is the single most important intellectual task of this generation, and leading is the most needed skill. The reason is simple. Leaders play a major role in helping us shape our life. Leaders define business and its practice. They determine the character of society. They define our teams, groups and communities. They set and administer government policy. In all walks of life, leaders' behaviors set the course others follow and determine the measures used to account for group actions.

Success in the new millennium, as in the past, will depend on how well leaders understand their roles, the leadership process and their own values and vision as well as those of their groups. Their behaviors set the course others follow and determine the values and other measures used to account for group actions.

Understanding leadership is, like all of the important aspects of life, a thing of the mind more than an objective reality. Traditionally, leadership has been thought of in terms of the heads, or chief officers of organizations, regardless of the tasks or functions they may perform. It is easy to think about leaders and leadership in terms of authority and headship and to talk about leadership as management. Some leaders are charged with insuring that a program of activities is carried out, assignments made and reports prepared and delivered on time (Mintzberg, 1973).

In reality, these tasks more accurately define a managerial role, which is only a part of the total task of leadership. But, given the nature of modern society—an exploding information base, global markets, rapidly changing product demands, a diverse and demanding population and a labor pool composed of knowledge workers—traditional management will no longer work. We need a new type of chief executive officer (CEO), a team leader, a coach, a builder instead of a controlling manager. A new way to think about the role of the leader, a new kind of leadership, is needed.

THE LEADERSHIP MIND-SET

The stumbling blocks to understanding what leadership really is are, in part, due to the way we structure ideas and thinking. We simply have not yet developed thought processes to picture leadership as a distinct activity taking place in a specific environmental context. Available textbooks reflect a mind-set established over 100 years ago, one that places science, order and control (e.g., management) at the center of any definition of leadership.

Nevertheless, in the last decades of this century, leadership for some people has come to refer to the task of setting and replacing the values guiding the corporation and its people. Some current writers see it in terms of trust. For them, leaders create trust cultures. A few people are combining much of this current discussion and concluding that the task is spiritual, a function of the leader's concern for the whole person, the inner sense of spirituality felt by individual leaders and by group members. These writers counsel that leadership begins with understanding the leader's core self, for that core self establishes what is good and true and beautiful for them and other group members.

Each of these ideas describe a mind-set, or point of view, a personal reality, we might adopt as a way to make sense of the dynamic interactive process called leadership. Regardless of the focus, the mind-set we adopt orders our thinking and makes understanding easier. While in a given reality—whether we see it as management, values setting, trust building or a spiritual focus—we can understand leadership only in terms of the parameters of that point of view. Unless something extraordinary happens, we cannot accept other points of view as creditable. Practically speaking, each of us is locked into our current reality and need heroic measures to move out of it.

ALTERNATIVE WAYS TO THINK ABOUT LEADERSHIP

The idea that individuals develop unique ways of looking at the world and use this mind-set to define and measure their life is, of course, not a new one. This idea is, for example, central to the idea of cultural difference. Certainly cultural differences in member behavior are obvious to even the casual observer. People of different national (or ethnic, or religious, or corporate, or civic) backgrounds behave differently, measure success differently and value material and intellectual things differently.

As we move through life, we change those around us and are changed by them in direct relationship to our personal cultural viewpoint about any key idea, including leadership. Our own intellectual journey toward leadership may mirror the path others follow. Our individual perception of what leaders do is given meaning in the context of our unique present and past experiences as both leader and led. Accepting as valid any other understanding of leadership than our customary one is, obviously, beyond our experience and very difficult.

Leadership is objective. It is. We can see it in our lives and the lives of those around us. It is a part of every social situation in which we participate or observe as a spectator. However, each of us sees leadership differently. Both our definition and our measure of its utility is unique to us. Each of us applies what we perceive leadership to be from the perspective of our unique experience. We form a mind-set that guides our thinking and defines our reality.

We can conceive of our leadership mind-set in terms of increasingly complex levels of mental and emotional awareness. While we are in one reality we may understand less complex realities but not fully comprehend more complex ones. We may even think that that level of understanding is not even creditable. Thus, defining leadership is an intensely personal activity limited by our personal paradigms or our mental state of being, our unique mind-set.

The science of Virtual Reality is a useful metaphor, which helps us understand this notion of levels of awareness. Flowing out of the computer revolution, Virtual Reality hardware and software create a digital version of reality and project the individual into that environment. Virtual Reality is called virtual, because it appears to be real but is not. It is only a model of the real environment we live in, emphasizing only enough of its aspects to simulate the real thing.

Virtual Reality provides a way for people to visualize, manipulate and interact with simulated environments through artificial means. In Virtual Reality a "world" is created that exists entirely in the memory of a computer and in our perception as participants. Using the power of computers, we are able to enter and interact within a fabricated environment that in many ways is real to us.

We all live every day in virtual environments defined, not by computers, but by our ideas and experience. Like a Virtual Reality computer, our cumulative experience creates a mind-set that lets us see our world more globally than does our local experience. But, at the same time, it creates a kind of prison that constrains our freedom of action. The mental environment we construct both frees us to function within its parameters and limits our ability to think beyond its borders. Over time, our virtual environment will change as our experience changes. But while we are in one virtual reality we may not be able to even accept the idea that other realities exist or that they may be more useful to us.

The idea of alternative environmental realities is supported not only by computer and information theory but also by both the social sciences and psychology. Several contemporary models serve to illustrate the intellectual support for this view.

Cultural Change

Cultural differences in individual behavior are obvious to even the casual observer. Each of us filters our perceptions, our values and our experience though our unique culture. Part of the confusion and imprecision we see in the literature has to do with this personal cultural life filter through which we view leadership. As we move through life we change those around us and are changed by them. Our cultural biases are very often more important than the objective reality. Our individual perception of what leaders do is given meaning in the context of our cultural experiences as both leaders and followers of another's leadership. Accepting as valid any other understanding of leadership than our personal one is, obviously, beyond our own experience and impossible.

Paradigms

A currently popular pattern for understanding our particular mind-set is that of paradigms. Basically a paradigm is a set of rules groups adopt, often implicitly, that define the boundaries of the acceptable. They tell us how to behave in order to be successful. Our paradigm provides a model for how problems are solved, people are to be treated and individual and group actions interpreted.

Credited with popularizing paradigms in business, Joel Barker (1992) defines a paradigm as a set of organizational realities, such as values, beliefs, traditional practices, methods, tools, attitudes and behaviors. Members of a social group construct paradigms to integrate their thoughts, actions and practices. A leadership paradigm consists of the rules and standards as well as the accepted examples of leadership practice, laws, theories, applications and work relationships in a corporation or team.

As individuals progress, they may shift from one leadership paradigm to another. An example of paradigm shifts in business is the shift from production by craftsmen to mass production. A more recent shift can be seen in the move from mass production to lean production. Managers who advocate mass production and those who advocate a lean production system, like that of Toyota, think and act differently. Their different practices, beliefs, values and assumptions define their different paradigms.

As people shift from one paradigm to another, their ideas, values and beliefs will change and so will their actions and practices. This shift may require reeducation and retraining about management thought and practice. When many people's beliefs and actions change in concert within a corporation or group, Barker (1992) refers to the transformation as a "paradigm shift."

The power of paradigms is that they affect our ability to see the world. Quite literally, what is obvious to one person may be totally invisible to another. Thus, those people who see leadership as position-based cannot accept that it is rational for leaders to occupy positions in the middle or lower reaches of the organization. Similarly, people who see leadership as management cannot accept that it is plausible for leaders to deal with their followers' spiritual sides as well as their skills.

Barker (1992) contends that paradigm shifts open new conceptual territories. His research suggests that members imbued with the values and mores of the prevailing group culture do not often shift paradigms. The most likely person to change a paradigm is an outsider, someone who is not imbued with the prevailing paradigm. Paradigm shifters are the outsiders that homogeneous societies fear. Yet, in the fundamental and profound change that the innovators (outsiders) bring is the ability to solve problems that had been deemed unsolvable within the old paradigm.

Leadership is, among other things, a task of shifting the group's paradigm.

States of Being

Another interesting way to think about our leadership relationships with each other and the world is in terms of the work of Clare W. Graves (1970). Graves did not deal directly with leadership, but he did build an interpersonal relationships model that emphasized the power of individual values and personal perception, or point of view, in shaping our thought and action. Applying it to leadership promises to increase our collective understanding of leadership theory and practice.

According to Graves's theory, the human being can be thought of as an open system able to take from the environment and give back to it. He says we perceive the world based on the inputs we receive as open systems. He defined eight levels of human existence (or virtual environments), which are related in a hierarchy. His descriptions of each state of existence are beside the present point. What is important is that he concludes that the level of existence we are in determines our values and therefore our actions, our relationships and our measures of success for self and for others.

A person in a given level uses the mind-set of that level to solve problems and choose his course of action in relationships with others. His preferences for a style of leadership are appropriate to that reality. If he were in another level, he would act differently and use different values to judge the appropriateness of his own behavior and that of his fellows. The process of growth is a continual evolution into progressively higher levels of psychological existence. Growth is marked by progressive subordination of older lower-order behavioral systems to newer higher-level behavioral systems. People normally pass through each stage sequentially from lower to next higher to next higher and so on.

As healthy adults we move from one level to another level as our circumstances change. We do not automatically move from one level of existence to progressively higher levels. Some people arrive in one stage and cannot move to another. Some stay in one level for a time and regress to a lower order. Regardless of the level, when we are in a given level we have only the degree of freedom to think about an issue allowed by that level.

LEVELS OF LEADERSHIP

We all see leadership differently depending on our current level of psychological existence, our current paradigm, our current virtual environment. Other viewpoints than those descriptive of our current reality will be seen as wrong, incorrect, perhaps even inconceivable to us. We only grow to another level as our environmental circumstances change. That is, we will not move away from an understanding of leadership as mere headship or as managerial control until we accept that there may be other ways to think about and value the leadership task.

Different people can view a given example of leadership differently. That is, leadership may be the same—practiced in the same way for the same results, using the same technologies—but depending on how we look at it, we may see it in vastly different lights. How we see it depends on the reality we are in.

That has been my experience, and I dare say that of others. Over the years, I have passed through at least five levels of understanding about what leaders do and the leadership process. Initially my view of leadership was technical, scientific, procedural, and managerial. Later, I came to see leadership as only a function of excellent managerial performance. Still later, as I observed leaders getting others to do what they wanted done, without exercising control, my focus turned to the idea that leadership was a process of getting followers to share the leader's vision and values.

More recently, I expanded that idea to include the concept of leadership as a task of creating cultures that support high levels of interactive mutual trust. Neither shared values nor trust cultures seem to explain leader success. It is clear to me now that leadership is the job of transforming the core nature and character of the leader, the corporation and its workers. In this mind-set I can accept the kernel of truth in each of the other states of being. They all have value. Each contributes to and supports the progressively higher levels. All point to leadership as a function of spirit.

Which of these states of being, which virtual environment, you, the reader, bring to leadership will depend on your past experiences and cumulative wisdom. Only time will tell which is the authentic truth. However, each virtual environment incrementally adds to our collective insight about the leadership task. Reading about those leadership virtual environments that seem extreme, or even ridiculous, may be interesting and educational. Gaining the knowledge may even be an event sufficient to move you to another state, another virtual reality relative to leadership.

While there is a kind of evolutionary order to our understanding, each leadership virtual reality has adherents today. They can be ranked hierarchically along a continuum from managerial control to spiritual holism. The five virtual environments include the following:

Leadership as Management

Leadership as Excellent (Good) Management

Values Leadership

Trust Cultural Leadership

Spiritual (Whole-Soul) Leadership.

Leadership as Management

Management is a role heads of organizations assume involving control over others' behaviors and actions. People who accept this conception of leadership truth center on the leader's management role. It conjures up ideas like controlling interpersonal relations, making decisions, aligning individual member actions and perceptions with corporate goals, planning, budgeting and directing the effort of the several followers engaged in the work. The manager role involves leaders in insuring that group activity is timed, controlled and predictable.

Since Frederick W. Taylor defined Scientific Management in 1911, many people have focused on the "hard sciences" techniques in describing both leadership and management. We have imposed a hard science behavioral focus on all human activities, including management activities. The effort has been to make leadership a science: controlled, precise, predictable. This science-focus has dictated leadership theory, method and practice—if not in the real world, surely in the literature.

Chronologically, leadership as management is the first modern virtual environment about leadership. It has been tested in controlled as well as real-world situations. Its utility is evaluated daily. It has been found wanting in some important respects. Presently available hard science leadership models are not satisfactory. They define leadership in substantially the same terms used to define management, adding to the confusion, rather than clarifying these two ideas. And they raise about as many questions as they answer.

Leadership as Excellent (Good) Management

Accepting the pull of the quality movement, another virtual environment emphasizes high-quality, excellent management as the real function of leadership. Today's excellent leaders do all that managers do with a quality focus that gives confidence to the rest of the organization. They have a positive attitude stemming from a belief in high-quality individual and group activity. They are catalysts—bringing out the best in workers, fostering worker innovation and igniting creativity. The quality movement changes the leader's perception of the follower core's character, provides a single focus for collective action and enlarges the domain of the leader.

A focus on quality is a focus on just one aspect of the managerial task. While a helpful way to look at managerial work, it does not deal directly with what many are beginning to define as better, more comprehensive approaches to understanding leadership. It does, however, introduce the careful reader to some of the core values that have guided leaders throughout time, like quality, concern for excellence, stakeholder development and values of integrity, caring, creativity and service. These form a basis for a more current theory.

Values Leadership

Breaking new ground in our journey to the truth about leadership is the idea that leaders set and enforce values for the group. The key idea in this virtual environment is simple: everybody has values, and these values trigger their behavior. If the leader wants to lead others, he or she must first insure that the group shares values in common and that these values provide both the goals (the group vision) and the measures of group and individual success.

This new conception of leadership proposes a kind of leadership rooted in the reality of human nature and conduct. It accepts the idea that individual and group action is values-driven. Its purposes rank individual change and development as equal to group productivity. It is worldwide in its application. In America its central characteristic is reliance on a few founding values that celebrate the individual. Values leadership moves beyond science to philosophy. It introduces a new leadership technology and new skills that are different in material ways from those that managers must acquire.

The virtual environment of values leadership makes full use of this truism. The leadership that will work today—and has always worked best in the past—is leadership based on shared values. The idea of values-based leadership is not new. The problem is we have not *thought* of our leadership in values terms. So the *idea* of values leadership is "new," while the *practice* is much more common.

Trust Cultural Leadership

Just as values shape the culture, so too does the culture shape leadership. The style of leadership leaders adopt (though not necessarily consciously) grows out of their ideas and feelings about the nature of man. A logical extension of the virtual environment of values leadership is the idea that the leader's task is to build a culture of shared values where people can come to trust each other enough to work together. Leadership is both an individual and a collective activity. Full understanding of leadership takes place only in cultures characterized by shared values and goals. Only in harmonious cultures can leaders impact their followers in assured ways.

People in this leadership virtual environment see the need for a unified, effective, harmonious culture characterized by mutual trust that allows leadership to take place. Indeed, leadership can only take place within a context where both leaders and followers can be free to trust the purposes, actions and intent of others.

The trust culture virtual environment of leadership sees the leader's role as not so much a characteristic of the individual leader as a condition of the culture he or she creates. While leadership may be spontaneous at times, most often it is a result of specific planned actions to create an environment conducive to internal harmony around values and ideals the leader and follower share or come to share. Leadership becomes a task of both impacting followers individually and influencing them as groups through shared cultural visions, values and behavior patterns.

Trust is central to leadership in organizations because followers are people who *choose* to follow leaders. They are not forced to do so. The trust of followers lets leaders lead. It is the glue holding the organization and its programs and people together. Indeed, no organization can take place without interpersonal trust. And, leaders cannot ignore the powerful element of trust as they go about creating and managing their organization's culture and inducing stakeholders to behave in needed ways.

Spiritual (Whole-Soul) Leadership

In the last decade of the twentieth century we can detect a new virtual environment that helps us understand leadership. A few people are combining much of the discussion of the past 15 or 20 years and concluding that leadership is a function of the leader's concern for the whole-soul, the inner self. They believe that leadership comes out of the leader's inner core spirit. This, not facts about personality or situation, determines what is right and good for them and for other organization members.

Even the casual observer can see some of the basis for this new way of thinking. Today people are hungry for meaning in their lives. They feel they have lost something, and they don't remember what it is they've lost. This has left a gaping hole in their lives. To fill this void, some are trying to blend their spiritual with their everyday work lives (Kantrowitz, 1994).

We have long known of the powerful, if implicit, impact of the spirit on decisions affecting our work. It is unmistakable, if only tangentially mentioned, in more and more public discussion. The reader may be aware, for example, of the "high touch" reaction to the introduction of high technology that John Naisbitt discussed as far back as 1982. The most recent pressures toward reinvention of the organization are clearly partially intended to invent corporate structures that recognize and respond to human needs for self expression. Whether it is a fad or a sea-change, the discernable shift in America from leadership based on control over resources to concern for the whole person is apparent.

Evidence is amassing that suggests that there is a significant connection between a leader's (or worker's) ability to have a transformational effect on the organization and his or her disposition towards spirituality. In the author's research 84 percent of surveyed managers confirmed this link (Fairholm, 1997). The reasons are obvious. Leaders or members who have a clear sense of their own spirituality and that of their coworkers can have a greater transformational effect on the organization, its forms, structures and processes than a formal reorganization plan.

And too, we cannot separate the person's spirituality from his or her actions and disposition. As coworkers see our communications are laced with commonly held core spiritual values, our statements will strike a responsive chord in these others and foster mutual growth. Failure to communicate our spiritual self will result in loss. Spirituality is the source of our most powerful and personal values. When leader and led can share core spiritual values, such as trust, faith, honesty, justice, freedom and caring, in the workplace, a true metamorphosis occurs and the corporation can reach new creative heights.

Leaders need followers to lead, but they need enabled people who are able to flourish in an environment of interactive trust, shared vision and common values. Leaders who are comfortable with themselves as happy and strong and can convey these qualities to others. They can, in this way, be a part of the spirituality of others. When this bonding is present, leaders and group members can be very effective.

SUMMARY

The reality we adopt to understand leadership is personal. It is selected as we experience leadership, and read about it and think about it. But the way we think, the point of view we develop out of our reading and experience, both illuminates and shades our understanding. Five mental models, or virtual environments, mark the 100-year progress of intellectual thought to full understanding of leadership. Each model is true in the sense that it helps describe some part of the leadership task. Each lays out a logical, rational pattern of leader action. But it is only together that they define the full picture.

Perhaps each of us has to move through each virtual leadership environment, accepting one for a while before we are ready to experience the next. This book is intended to help the traveler see the landmarks guiding this movement. It is also intended to raise the possibility that the trail you are now on is not the only one, maybe not the best to meet your leadership needs in the twenty-first century.

PART I

Leadership as Management

Management, as a role for heads of organizations, involves control over others' behaviors and actions. For most people a position of leadership centers around the management role, its tasks and techniques—its technology. It conjures up ideas like controlling interpersonal relations, making decisions, aligning individual member actions and perceptions with corporate goals, planning, budgeting and directing the effort of the several followers engaged in the work with us. The manager role involves insuring that group activity is timed, controlled and predictable.

The idea of business management is pervasive and powerful in society. It defines those human attributes thought appropriate to success in the formal corporation, like competition, ambition and financial astuteness. The Western myth of managerial man is one of the dominant myths of our age. The central feature of this concept is the idea of management. In the early days of this century (and even today), management was given prominence over other, some arguably more important, human activities related to emotional needs, wider family relationships and social or intellectual aspirations. For many, management has become the metaphor of the twentieth century, encompassing work, workers and work cultures.

1

Evolution of the Manager as Leader

Leadership is the oldest (organizational) profession. Management is the second oldest. The heads of the first social groups led because they possessed the following kinds of personal characteristics—they were the biggest, strongest, smartest, the best dressed. And, they were believed to have the ear of the gods. Today most people would associate these characteristics with leadership. It was only later, when social groups became larger and more complex, that these head people began to move away from this personal kind of leadership to impersonal, objective management of the group's resources.

Modern professional management has come of age in the twentieth century. The past 100 years have seen professionalism come to the management of all of our social institutions. As expected, the precedent of this recent history conditions much of the current thinking about leadership. To understand what leadership is and the nature of its development, we must first understand its management roots.

To consider properly the work of the manager, it is necessary to put the function of management in context within an organization. Many attempts have been made to break down and define the work of leaders and set up a model of management. In the late nineteenth century, the sociologist Max Weber, after extensive study, offered the bureaucratic model as the best system of management for the rapidly expanding German economy. At the turn of the twentieth century, Henri Fayol, after studying the best organizations, reduced the work of managers to a series of universal laws. In 1937 Luther Gulick and Lyndall Urwick summarized the work of the manager into seven universal functions, like planning, budgeting and decision making.

The problem with these, and many other attempts to define the function of leadership in terms of the manager's work, is that they emphasize that one aspect of the overall task to the exclusion of the complete picture (Mintzberg, 1973). Management alone gives only a vague indication of the actual work of leaders. Simple observation supports a contention that leaders do not merely plan, direct and budget. In studies of general managers conducted by John Kotter (1991), he found that they spent much of their time interacting orally with others. The manager's activities were often unplanned and the result of diversions such as unscheduled meetings and telephone calls (Kotter, 1991). The conversations tended to be short, disjointed and to touch on a number of issues. These observational data support the idea that acting in their role allows managers to influence the actions of others in more than just functional, systemic or procedural ways.

And, too, national, even global, concerns affecting our society help shape the current challenge to better, more directed leadership. Changes in population, culture, economics and other factors are global. These pressures supersede discrete institutional boundaries. They override the parochial parameters of traditional theory and contemporary practice of corporate management and leadership. Past theories of leadership based on management theory cannot sustain this assault. Yet, leadership as management was the foundation for much of the theory building about leadership until the last two decades of the twentieth century. It still affects leadership theory.

Initial efforts to discuss leadership placed it as a task of management. Leadership was seen as one of many skills the competent individual must master if he or she wants to inspire others to full professional competence. Leadership was, heretofore, just another task managers needed to become expert in, much like budgeting, organizing or personnel management. Careful reading of the literature identifies several distinct models of managerial competencies that early writers associated with the managerial task of leadership. Each adds something to our understanding of what the manager needs to know and to be to attain success. The locus of managerial leadership is at the chief officer level—whatever the title the organization gives its chief officers.

For many people management is leadership. For them, leadership centers on management tasks and techniques. The manager role involves leaders in insuring that group activity is timed, controlled and programmed. Lumping these operational tasks under the name "leadership" has some merit. One part of leadership has to do with accomplishing organizational objectives and developing the behavioral skills to get others to do the organization's work, to be productive. But we cannot think that being scrupulously accurate in computing profit or loss, or insuring that the letter of the procedure is adhered to, is all that is needed. Management tasks are intellectual skills-based tasks requiring the organization head to learn how to manage others and know the laws, rules and procedures, and the tools, needs and requirements for program success.

Of course there is value in understanding these control tools: the "mind of leadership." Each of us develops over time a *virtual environment* that catalogs and interrelates the sum of our experience into patterns or theories of practice that help us make sense of our experience. The mind of leadership reflects life experiences and systematizes them into strategies that guide action. Applied to our business concerns, this reality represents the intellectualized foundations of our experience, our expertise.

The managerial "mind" of leadership is critical to day-to-day success. Some routine behavior, some system, is necessary in certain circumstances; some techniques work better than others do in a given situation. Knowing these tools and becoming expert in their use is important. Knowing which rule to follow, which tool to use, can help us attain success. This is important, but it is only a part of the task of the leader. Just getting the work done and reporting in a timely manner— difficult as this sometimes is—is not all that is required.

Since Frederick W. Taylor invented Scientific Management at the turn of the century, we have focused on techniques of management based on the scientific method. We have imposed a hard science behavioral focus on most human activities, including management activities. The effort has been to make management a science: measurable, precise and repeatable. This scientific focus has dictated management theory, method and practice—at least in the literature—for a generation.

Leadership, too, has fallen victim to the pull of the scientific method because some see leadership as just another tool or skill of management. Even those who see it as a separate function have used hard-science techniques to build their theories. And they have assumed hard-science goals of precision and predictability as the desired outcome measures. Early definitions of leadership mirrored those of management in theory, process and goals.

This need was filled in the change from personal charismatic leadership to imposition of management control. Management relies on internal logical consistency, repeatability and subordination of the many to the few. In all of our social institutions—the military, industry and the church—the movement has been away from the inconstant individual leader to the stable, predictable, logically focused manager— from the minister of policy to the administrator of programs.

We have kept (albeit in adapted forms) the ceremonies, procedures and customs that have served to keep subordinates at a respectful psychological distance. Where the ancient leader once held symbols of power, managers now hold them. Today's managers have adopted the ceremonial robes and perquisites that were formerly assumed by tribal chiefs, priests and generals. These almost sacred leadership symbols have only been changed to conform to the needs of modern managers and contemporary civilization. Today instead of fancy robes, headdresses and mystic ceremonies, we see them today in academic gowns, perquisites of office, $1,500 business suits, showy offices and the fostered illusion that the manager has "the word" and is the centerpiece of the communication network.

What has taken place in the modern corporation over the past century is a shift from leadership to management. This is the same shift that we have seen in the decline and fall of the ancient church, the Roman Imperial Army and most older social institutions. The obvious intent is the same in both systems, to produce respect and obedience in subordinates. The perquisites of managerial power inspire a decent awe for the professional manager (or teacher, or lawyer or doctor, etc.). They add an air of pseudo-sacred solemnity and mystery to replace our innate needs for inspiration.

For most of this century headship was seen as much more of a matter of ceremony than of personality and vision. The logistics expert has supplanted the charismatic hero in the military. In government, the shift has been from the appointed, hereditary or revolutionary leaders to the calculating, power-preserving, authoritarian master-bureaucratic managers of today. The religious prophet has been replaced by the managerial bishop. We have come to distrust charismatic powers in every aspect of society and have replaced them with pseudo-ceremonies that can be timed, organized and controlled.

The fall of leadership and the rise of modern management have brought mixed results. This trend has allowed us to attain remarkable material progress. Modern management has produced fantastically complex organizations, which are able to cope with the pluralistic needs and desires of a growing and demanding population. But the costs are also significant. Without the bonding true leadership produces, we have created a working population characterized by anomie, alienation and despair. Our measures of productivity in our organizations and in our society as a whole are down, morale is low, and creativity is off.

Management can produce tangible things extraordinarily well. It is less adept at producing motivated, inspired, people. We cannot manage people into the commitment necessary to accept the risks of battle, for example, or any other significant social enterprise. We can only lead them in these life-changing social activities. Managers are not trained, and their systems and theories are not geared to independent follower action. Rather, managers are successful if they can direct desired behavior, control deviation and punish recalcitrance.

This propensity for control through uniformity is seen in our organizational structures, operating systems, reports and management approaches. But as the authority of management spreads over the organization, quality deteriorates. Management shuns excellence. It feeds on repeatable performance geared to the lowest skilled employee. It feeds on controlled (and controllable) mediocrity.

In contrast to the evolution of management over the ages, modern management theory has a short history. Its beginnings date only to the period around the turn of the century. We date our understanding of leadership as management from this period. Early management theory developed as a set of principles and practices the workmanlike practice of which was predictive of success in getting other people to do the organization's work.

Initial attempts to formulate a coherent statement of management theory were based on the assumption that there are common principles underlying managerial success, whatever the field within which management is practiced. That is, management must be thought of as being generic and universal. This was the essential tenant of Scientific Management.

SCIENTIFIC MANAGEMENT

Frederick W. Taylor (1911) is generally acknowledged to be the father of the Scientific Management movement. He equated leadership with effective management. His central focus was on productivity improvement and efficiency. Scientific Management is unique not so much in its central purposes, but in the technologies by which it attempted to achieve efficiencies. The techniques in Scientific Management reflect Taylor's belief that planning needs to be separated from doing. Taylor suggested that managerial excellence made managers stand out among their subordinates and peers.

Taylor applied the methods of the hard sciences to the problems of attaining management efficiencies. He relied, therefore, on observation, measurement and experimentation to help solve production and control problems. He relied also on incentives to attract workers and keep them working at high levels of effort. Scientific study of production processes and the payment of high wages, he said, could best solve industrial efficiency issues. That is, the most efficient work will be done when managers design work methods based on scientific research and pay workers high wages to insure that workers use scientifically developed work methods.

Detailed analysis, careful observation of work done by the best workers and close measurement of work steps would produce the optimal standard practices and working conditions. Standardizing work in terms of carefully designed standard operating procedures insured that both levels of production and quality were maintained. Managers had the responsibility to develop these standard practices. They were also charged under Scientific Management with recruiting, training and then supervising workers, using elaborate incentive systems to induce them to perform within the confines of these scientific techniques.

Taylor and the early scientific managers developed much of the quality control and general management technologies and techniques used by today's managers. Scientific managers developed time study, motion study and work measurement. They developed systems for laying out optimal work stations; and established work standards, control desks, production control charts and most other control systems and tools still in use today. The range of management systems introduced since Taylor's time that focus on task and quantity issues of management, including operations research, management science and statistical quality control, trace their origins to the Scientific Management movement.

Other researchers contributed to, and made fashionable, various versions of Scientific Management. In the early decades of this century one of the most popular was a model of the manager's job that divided the tasks of management into seven distinct functions. Credited to Luther Guilick and British researcher Lyndall Urwick (1937), Organization and Methods (or simply OM) centered our thinking on seven tasks managers perform summarized under the mnemonic POSDCORB:

P   lanning
  O   rganizing
    S   taffing
      D   irection
        CO   ordination
          R   eporting
            B   udgeting

The skills defined by this POSDCORB model are technical. Managers became known by their specialty. Thus, we see managers as budgeteers, personnelists and supervisors. The theoretical basis was Scientific Management or later versions of it like decision theory, statistical decision making, management science and some versions of human relations theory. The virtue of this model is its clarity and simplicity. The manager's job can be conveniently divided up into actions to further one or more of these functions. That is what, the theory said, managers do.

Supplementing Taylor's focus on task and technique, Henri Fayol (1949), a French scientific manager of the same period, concentrated on the generic functions of management. He categorized managerial work into six organizational activities or functions: technical, commercial, financial, security, accounting and managerial. He also identified a number of principles of management. They include

- Division of Work (specialization of labor)
- Authority and Responsibility
- Discipline
- Unity of Command (each employee reports to only one boss)
- Unity of Direction
- Subordination of Individual interest to the General Interest
- Remuneration of Personnel
- Centralization
- Scalar (Hierarchical) Chain
- Order (everything in its proper place)
- Equity
- Stability of Tenure of Personnel
- Initiative (thinking and then executing a plan)
- Esprit de Corps

Fayol touted these principles of management as universal principles effective in any organization in any field.

Following the work of Fayol, the principles approach to management focused upon managerial activities or functions guided by universal principles. These principles affect those tasks essential to attaining corporate objectives. The major managerial functions are planning, organizing, directing, controlling and deciding. Other functions are also identified in this body of research, but these five seem to be most commonly mentioned.

Management functions should not be confused with organizational functions such as finance, production, engineering, sales and marketing. These deal with organizational processes, whereas the managerial functions relate more directly to the actions of individual managers. Managerial functions can and are performed by managers assigned to each of the functional areas. Thus planning, organizing, directing, controlling and deciding occurs in each of the production, engineering, finance, sales and marketing units.

Managerial functions are also distinct from a variety of technical functions that are ongoing in any organization. These non-managerial tasks are critical to success and are usually delegated to subordinates. They include tasks like scheduling, auditing, reporting and measuring. Of course, managers may perform these tasks themselves, but when doing so are not involved in management.

Position or title is not as important in defining managerial work as is the nature of the work actually done by the incumbent. Thus, a non-manager may perform managerial tasks like planning. When doing that work, the employee is performing a managerial function. Similarly, a manager may schedule workers and work and thus be engaged in the technical function of scheduling. In either case, the work done, not the title held, determines whether the person is functioning as a manager or a technician.

Planning

Logically, planning precedes the other managerial functions. It is the first step of identification of the organization's objectives and development of action plans to accomplish them. Planning includes development of strategic objectives; data collection about past, present and projected future organizational effort, markets and clientele groups; and creation of necessary policies and procedures and methods to turn plans into reality.

Setting Objectives

Corporate objectives identify the purposes and goals sought by a unit and its management team. Each corporate unit sets its own objectives, some of which may be incompatible with those of other units or other stakeholders. While it is difficult to identify ultimate organizational goals, all organizations share in some way the goals of (1) profit, (2) survival, (3) growth and (4) service to stakeholders.

Organizing

The organizational chart reflects the results of the managerial function of organizing. The tasks involved include grouping like activities, assigning operating authority and placing responsibility for organizational functions and technical tasks. Organizing deals with the formal relationships present within the organization which constitute the organization itself. It is often pictured graphically as a diagram that groups activities and connects them via authority relationships and sometimes certain communications channels.

Directing

Direction engages the manager in guiding and supervising subordinates toward the realization of the team's goals. This function asks managers to be conversant with human relations theory and specific technologies like communications, employee development, conflict resolution and motivation. Directing also asks managers to be familiar with the older Scientific Management ideas of incentive pay. Increasingly the function is seen as a motivational one, which uses both physical and psychological rewards to insure desired worker performance.

Controlling

Controlling is the task of evaluating performance, determining technique and applying necessary corrective measures. The control process includes steps such as establishing standards, comparing actual performance with these standards and taking corrective actions. The intent is to establish strategic control points along the work process and develop reporting and measuring systems to assess these critical parts of the entire process. Standards set include those of quality, quantity, cost, and time and material use.

Deciding

In each of these managerial functions choices have to be made as to what to do or not do. Managers decide, make choices about what they should do, what employees should do and what the organization should do. Decision making is a defining function. It is, perhaps, the quintessential managerial function. Our decisions determine what and who we are as people and as a corporation. It involves the choice itself as well as the tasks of determining desired outcomes, data collection, analysis of alternative decision points and followup to determine if decisions made did in fact produce desired results.

BEHAVIORAL SCIENCE APPROACHES

Early work in leadership as management also included consideration of a behavioral approach. This model applies the methods and findings of psychology, social psychology, sociology and anthropology to help understand organizational behavior. The most famous and significant behavioral science approach occurred in the series of experiments at the

Hawthorne, Illinois plant of the Western Electric Company during the late 1920s and early 1930s. These so-called Hawthorne studies (Mayo, 1993) initially sought to further test Scientific Management ideas. They began by investigating the relationship between physical conditions of the workplace and employee productivity. They soon found that the social variables between researchers and the worker subjects were more important than the physical variables within which they worked as factors affecting productivity.

This unexpected outcome inspired widespread study of human behavior in the workplace. Elton Mayo (1993), a principal consultant in the Hawthorne studies, is generally considered to be the founder of the field of industrial and human relations. For Mayo, rather than being a hindrance in productivity, human relations became a broad new field of study in order to improve both morale and productivity. The manager-as-leader now needed to be expert in another new technology, the science of human relations.

Behavioral science studies in part expanded traditional Scientific Management and in part conflicted with some defined principles. They also added new factors to the mix of issues facing the leader-manager. For example, piecework systems often led to conflicts between workers and time and motion study experts. These studies also found that, in addition to being a formal arrangement of functions, the firm is a complex social system whose success depends on the appropriate application of behavioral science principles.

Leaders imbued with this leadership philosophy soon saw employee satisfaction and morale as prime goals to be sought. The underlying assumption was that high morale leads to high productivity. Later research indicated that this assumption was oversimplified. Behavioral science approaches also include motivation study, see the organization as a social system, consider the impact of informal as well as formal corporate structures and identify leadership and its relationship to corporate success.

With the addition of leadership studies to the behavioral science approach to management, researchers entered a new dimension. They began the formal process of studying the organization as a complex of employee motivation. They began to view the corporation as both a social and a technical system and to study the process of interpersonal communications and employee development. Leadership studies, which began in the early decades of the twentieth century, have maintained these early intellectual roots.

In the 1970s Henry Mintzberg (1973) challenged again the models based on Scientific Management. In his experience, managers did not *do* POSDCORB functions. They did something else as they accomplished such tasks as planning and organizing. Mintzberg gave us two sets of ideas to use in thinking about, describing and training for management. The first was a set of characteristics of managerial work that apply to all processes and functions. The second was a listing of descriptive tasks all managers perform for their organizations. Mintzberg's listing includes six job characteristics:

1. Managers produce a great quantity of work at an unrelenting pace.
2. They favor variety, fragmentation and brevity.
3. They prefer specific, explicit issues that are on the current agenda, not long-term seminal issues.
4. Managers are at the center of a communication network of contacts.
5. They prefer verbal media in communicating.
6. They seek to be in control of their own affairs.

Mintzberg also identified ten managerial tasks divided into three functional areas:

- INTERPERSONAL ROLES: Figurehead, Leader, Liaison
- INFORMATIONAL ROLES: Nerve Center (focal point for the communication network), Disseminator, Spokesman
- DECISIONAL ROLES: Entrepreneur, Disturbance Handler, Negotiator, Resource Allocator

Mintzberg defined skills managers need that are more complex than the simple POSDCORB tasks. They are political skills requiring negotiation and compromise; technical skills of accurate communication; behavioral skills of coordination, conflict resolution and innovation; and creative skills. Mintzberg's model is clearly behavioral. But, intellectually and operationally, it is still fully in the orbit of Scientific Management and sees the leader in terms of managerial control.

SYSTEMS MANAGEMENT AND QUANTITATIVE MANAGEMENT

Following on the pure study of management as a system of control, the systems approach is a more recent contributor to management theory and technology. The historical event that triggered this approach to management was the development during World War II of Operations Research (OR) by the British military services. OR's most enduring contribution was in legitimizing systems theory.

The system approach lets researchers take primary interest in studying whole situations and relationships, rather than organizational units and other small segments. Systems theorists see the whole corporation as not just a series of functions like production, sales, engineering and accounting. Productivity improvement, for them, is a function of the interaction of all components, not an incremental improvement of individual segments.

It is important to note that for this body of researchers, a system could mean a social system and thus have a behavioral orientation. It could also mean a technical system and have a Scientific Management focus. Operations Research introduced statistical quality control and other quantitative management models into the discussion of management. The focus here is not so much on employee motivation, conflict resolution and communications as it is on decision making in these areas.

Developed over the years since World War II, systems theory includes an interest in the mathematical models and quantitative techniques associated with operations research. It has also resulted in viewing the corporation as an interrelated decision-making system connected by communications channels directing information to decision-points within the organization. The systems approach tends to view the corporation in information flow terms and the leader in technical, procedural terms.

Coming out of this branch of early management theory and practice are several techniques and tools that are still used and are still descriptive of this approach to management. Program Evaluation and Review Technique (PERT) is one. PERT is a planning and control method that is fully within the systems approach and used to control complex production systems. This approach cuts across functional departments to provide leaders with detailed information about project status during all phases of design, production and distribution. Critical Path Method (CPM) is a similar tool familiar to many scientific managers in late twentieth century America and the industrialized world.

ORGANIZATIONAL STRUCTURE AND MANAGEMENT

The environments within which most people work are the firm, the corporation and the work teams within them. We model the modern large-scale (and more and more, the not so large-scale) organization after the classical bureaucracy, which is highly structured and geared to the production of tangible objects. In many respects, life in large-scale organizations sometimes resembles life in a totalitarian state. Workers are labor bondservants of the managers who control their lives in a detailed fashion. In business organizations as in governments, however, totalitarianism is incompatible with high performance.

Few leaders do more than coordinate efforts in their small sphere, with no one caring about what anyone else is doing (Adair, 1985). Management has come to consist mostly of mechanistic skills. It is no more sufficient to sophisticated workers today than serfdom was to the factory work of the early Industrial Revolution. Indeed, the corporation and other large employers may be among the last bastions of a stifling bureaucratic dictatorship.

Today we are moving beyond bureaucracy to rebuild the patterns of our formal relationships. The focus now is on the quality of our corporate communications as the basis of freedom and rights (Pinchot and Pinchot, 1994). We no longer see workers as just objects. Bureaucracy is defined by chains of dominance and submission. Initiative means asking for permission. Most workers get to use only a tiny fraction of their potential. The freedom of speech essential to adaptation to rapid change is at the sufferance of the boss. Bosses tell employees where they will work, what they will do, how to do it.

Some of the stress that workers feel today in the modern corporation may be due to this obsolete structural form. Bureaucracy produces only simple and shortsighted answers in an era when anticipating interconnections and dealing with long-term implications is a requirement for survival. Changing bureaucratic structure does not mean only rearranging organization charts. It begins with liberating the self-organizing potential of working people so they can work in constantly changing units. Management theory and its version of leadership do not do this.

Unit leaders guide today's well-managed companies. The core responsibility of the executive is to be an effective leader for the team. Spirit supports and sustains each person in the team. The most effective leaders, therefore, are those who create a team spirit that makes the work exciting. For example, the mark of Lee Iacocca's success at Chrysler Corporation was that from the beginning he started building a team approach at every level. Indeed, unity was a key point in his outstanding leadership style.

Today we measure all that we consider important in monetary terms. Indeed, our measurement systems are keyed to a monetary standard. Accounting, auditing, control and success itself, all are defined, measured, compared in terms of a standard unit: money. We define any other values as ephemeral, irrelevant. Control over money makes managers successful. By converting all activity to money (numbers), we can compare, control and prescribe everything, which then can be processed, computerized, handled—in short, managed. The manager knows the price of everything. Monetary cost is the prime value of management.

Worldwide, executives are realizing the need for something better to reach their company's and their people's potential. To meet today's challenging markets and increased competition, many managers are becoming more involved in the daily activity of corporate life. They are encouraging honest communication between management and staff. They recognize that happiness is the purpose of life—social and business life, and that it occupies the time and energies of all workers. It is something natural and desirable; when we recognize and foster it, it can be helpful in improving all aspects of corporate work life—at the bottom line and elsewhere throughout the organization.

The non-countable features of the corporation are the realm of the true leader.

2

Purposes of Management

Writers in the field of management regard coordination as a main objective of management rather than as just another function. Coordination is a byproduct of hierarchy. There can be no coordination without subordination. Successful coordinating activities follow from effectively carrying out the functions of planning, organizing, directing, deciding and controlling. These functions result from the formal allocation of authority within organizations. Lack of coordination between corporate units may result from incompatible policies and procedures. Failure to define authority relationships clearly may also result in a lack of coordination of efforts. Similarly, when managers fail to decide, control their resources effectively or provide direction, it is impossible to predict that the corporate unit will function in a coordinated fashion.

Seeing leadership in managerial terms adds additional purposes to the tasks of management. For example, people also relate themselves with any organization in order to satisfy their own objectives. Unless the corporation in doing its work also provides an opportunity for stakeholders to satisfy their individual objectives, it will not be able to fully satisfy its own goals. Owners, managers, employees, suppliers and customer groups all seek their individual objectives through their association with the organization. The prime task of managerial planning is to set objectives that will help the organization survive, prosper and meet the needs of all stakeholders.

Without the contributions of each group, effective organizational action would be impossible. A primary task of managerial leaders is to allocate available resources so that a balance is achieved among the competing interests of the several groups of stakeholders represented. Meeting the objectives of some stakeholders and not others would result in reduced effectiveness or, even, dissolution of the organization itself. All objectives sought by all stakeholders are of importance to the manager-leader.

MODERN FUNCTIONS OF MANAGEMENT

For a hundred years management practice has been things- rather than people-oriented. While effective in meeting production-of-things tasks, this practice may not be useful in the large-scale organizations in which we work today, which do not engage as much in the production of tangible objects. Much of today's work is to produce information, facts and ideas. The people—the knowledge workers—creating and using these facts want involvement. They want to manage their own work lives and contribute to their own level of competence, whether or not they are in a leadership position.

Obviously, the traditional corporation doesn't lend itself to the manipulation of ideas or broad involvement in planning and decision making. Manipulation of knowledge requires flexibility, adaptability and sometimes even waste. Bureaucracies, on the other hand, fight waste by sponsoring programs of efficiency and tight supervisory control. Current management and structural models are incompatible with this new push for self-determination by workers and today's unique customer demands for products and services.

Plainly, work is changing (Pinchot and Pinchot, 1994). No longer do we need machine-like bureaucratic procedures. Rather, the movement is from unskilled work to knowledge work and from individual work to teamwork. We are replacing meaningless, repetitive tasks with innovative ones. We now ask our workers—and they are asking their leaders—to move from a system that once required of them single-skilled expertise to one that requires many skills. Power is moving away from supervisors and to customers. We are replacing coordination from above with cooperation among peers.

The role of the middle-manager—perhaps the most endangered species of worker in large-scale organizations today—has changed. It has moved from authoritarian straw boss through expert advisor and information conduit to coordinator of employee participation. The present circumstance has produced a situation where workers often do not need supervisors at all. The constant tension resulting from this condition of accelerating change places impossible pressures on traditional structures and on the people doing the work and their leaders. New methods, new leadership and new tools are needed.

The following contemporary functions seem to more accurately describe management today. They find their roots in early Scientific Management or human relations models. They offer insight into the human nature of both manager and subordinate and represent a melding of these two pioneering theories.

Objectives

Setting objectives is a formal management tool for balancing group objectives to achieve economic value for all stakeholders. Establishing a hierarchy of objectives lets managers allocate resources to all units in a planned and coherent way and with a greater expectation of organizational success. Managing based on the objectives of each organizational unit leader focuses on the economic contribution of each. Since each unit does different parts of the needed work, objectives will differ among units of an organization. Together they define the corporation's work effort and the outcomes desired by managers.

Change

Our virtual environment defines the rules of the games we play. It establishes and defines our boundaries of action and tells us how to successfully behave inside those boundaries (Barker, 1992). Change involves a shift in our virtual environments. Most people find this is difficult, even impossible, to even think about. Changing our virtual environment is a major transformation of our sense of self; this is usually accomplished by someone at the fringes of the organization—a marginal person. Barker called these people paradigm pioneers.

Trust

Trust can be increased by participation. Stakeholder boards, advisory boards, volunteers, and neighborhood councils can all help. Management by wandering around can also help develop trust. Frequent appearances at meetings of stakeholder groups also helps. Providing marketing services is another way to increase trust.

Nevertheless, distrust, not trust, is characteristic of many organizations today. Distrust can hamper excellence. Most people trust their immediate bosses but express concern about the general society. Many perceive their bosses to be insensitive and organizations to be indifferent to customers. One reason may be a low priority on service.

TQM—High-Quality Focus

The key to high quality is a change in mind-set to the idea of continuous improvement. Managers must lead, but all employees must also accept this vision. Attaining high quality is a journey, a process, not an event. (Aguayo, 1990). It is a new way of thinking about quality, a philosophy, more than a technique. Often it is a radical departure from traditional bureaucratic operations. It requires top management support and involvement, is often customer-driven, involves continuous improvement, is a participatory process and is not bound solely by the profit motive.

Several common themes are present in the quality-excellence literature. Remaining close to the customer is, perhaps, the most prominent. Encouraging employee involvement through empowerment, helping employees to take ownership and develop themselves as a part of their work relationships is also common. Other common themes are contracting with employees for performance, efforts to make more efficient use of resources and long-range strategic planning.

Performance Appraisal

Employee appraisal is intended to measure how well the individual employees function within the organization (Crane, Lantz and Shafritz, 1976). In appraising performance, managers measure individual work behavior. They define quality work, assess skills, document the basis for future promotions, administer discipline, manage superior-subordinate communications and determine pay and compensation. Performance measurement is usually based on personal traits or behavior. Deming (1986) denounced appraisal systems as one of the seven deadly sins of management and stated that their effect is devastating. They nourish short-term performance, annihilate long-term planning, build fear, demolish teamwork and nourish rivalry and politics. Appraisals produce negative consequences like:

- high costs
- deteriorating relationships
- decreased motivation
- potential litigation
- poor or false data
- loss of self esteem
- high turnover.

The real solutions to organizational improvement are likely to involve corporate culture, commitment and accountability.

Reassignment and Job Rotation

Job reassignment is defined as a way to enrich jobs (Grifin, 1991). It is closely related to job rotation—the systematic shifting of employees from one job to another with the goal of sustaining worker motivation and interest. John Gardner (1964) says job reassignment benefits people by providing them with new challenges, honing new skills and broadening experience. Ouchi (1981), in *Theory Z*, recommended reassignment, noting that it was as a major component of the lifelong career path followed by some Japanese companies.

Reassignment contributes to job satisfaction when it increases responsibility and authority. It is enabling. Reassignment works best when applied to managers. Reassignment is effective when there is a productive and challenged work force (Graham, 1994), when the organization has a strategy for growth and when reassignment is an option for workers at all levels in the organization.

Participation

Participation has always been a part of American life. Our early small town focus was on citizen leaders. Now size and complexity have made individual involvement difficult. Lack of participation has contributed to isolation, disengagement and distrust of leaders in all social and economic institutions. We need to distinguish between voluntary cooperation and compliance. Participation involves members in program planning and conduct, supporting those in authority above them and voluntarily obeying their instructions.

Motivation

Managers engage in motivation to help employees focus their minds and energies on doing their work as effectively as possible. It is not boosting enthusiasm in the firm or making employees *feel* happy. It is not a simple formula to make people more responsible or a bribery system. Rather motivation serves as a spark to stimulate, move, arouse and encourage employees to strive for a personal best, while nourishing specific corporate needs. Motivation includes some sort of reward system—a quid pro quo. It begins with strong interactive communications between mangers and employees.

Ethics

We live our lives in situations that reflect the fundamental character and disposition of a group. Our work (or other) environments delineate the ideals and values that inform group beliefs and practices. Ethics involves thinking systematically about these situations. It is about morals, attitudes and conduct and making judgements about right and wrong. Ethics implies a willingness to accept the consequences of one's actions. It refers to principles of action that implement or promote moral values. Ethics also involves politics, the active cooperation with others for common ends (Thompson, 1985).

Leadership as management is logical. It focuses on one important aspect of the task of getting others to do work the leader wants done. It is clear, specific and subject to control and verification. But in essence, it equates leadership and management as the same thing. And, given the economy of nature (and dictionaries), we can't stretch two meanings from one idea.

PART II

Leadership Excellence

The next virtual environment that dominated leadership theory in America involves a maturing of the idea of leadership. It is essentially an idea of emphasis rather than one of substance. It defines leadership as "good management." This virtual environment saw its greatest popularity in the 1970s. It thinks leadership is what "good" managers do. It focuses on performance excellence in managerial tasks. It centers on the leader's need to be sensitive to the human relations needs of workers along with the productivity demands on them. And it emphasizes elements in the working relationship between leaders and followers: a new concept of the manager-employee relationship.

Leaders concerned with quality, innovation and development of their people create excellent organizations. Excellence-focused leaders are mature horizon thinkers with a penchant for high-quality performance. They define their mission in terms of high quality and see leadership as broadly dispersed across the organization. They encourage the creative use of systems and resources, responding to the pressures of the environment and the potential of the future. This focus on excellence encompasses the leader's ideas about self, followers and the common corporate culture.

3

Leadership as Excellent Management

Following on the development of leadership as management came the
idea of leadership as good management. That is, people began to re-
strict leadership ideas to emphasize high-quality and excellent managerial performance. Unlike leadership as management, this virtual
environment does not focus solely on systems and control, operational
style or productivity. Rather, leadership as excellent management involves prioritizing innovation, concern for customers, quality and simple structures (Samuelson, 1984).

Gitlow and Gitlow (1987) described the pre-excellence state of management as being adrift without a rudder. Their solution was a return
to high quality, to altering the overall approach to managing our work
systems and work units to focus on high quality. Using the model of
Japanese industry, who used Deming's comprehensive quality approach, they predicted a similar rise in quality for American organizations. They and many others proffered plans to raise American
management (leadership) to its former greatness using a system of
quality improvement.

Leadership excellence has emerged as both a technology and a value
system. It is a virtual environment orientated toward the leader's role;
it defines this role in terms of service to others. Brassier (1985) also
defined it in strategic terms. It describes leaders who take confidence
in a commitment to the development of the capacities of people. These
leaders live by this principle of development.

The beauty of the idea of leadership excellence is its simplicity and common sense. Leadership excellence requires no gimmicks, no complicated theory or philosophy, no new funding, no great charisma. Evidence suggests that there are pockets of excellence in most organizations. They can be present in the most traditional productivity-oriented groups or in badly run organizations.

Interest in good (e.g., high-quality) management is, of course, not new. A focus on high-quality performance has always been a part of management and leadership. Lammermeyer's (1990) research points out that quality was a factor in the earliest management systems. He reports that these systems and processes actually have their origins in ancient rules, guild standards, trade agreements and formalized standard practices.

HISTORICAL THREADS OF THE QUEST FOR QUALITY

The present-day interest in leadership as a function of good management can trace its roots to the turn of the century interest in Scientific Management. The actual beginnings of the excellence movement can be traced into a much more ancient past. Long before modern management's current interest, older civilizations valued high quality in individual and group performance (George, 1968). The Phoenicians used a very effective corrective action program to maintain quality. They cut off the hand of the person responsible for unsatisfactory quality. According to Lammermeyer (1990), part of item 229 relating to Phoenician housing construction standards stated: "If a builder has built a house for a man and his work is not strong and the house falls in and kills the householder, that builder shall be slain." Even our most fanatical advocates of high quality have not yet reached this level of urgency.

Guilds in the Middle Ages were the first counterparts of modern Quality Circles, small groups of employees tasked to improve group operations. Guild members ate their midday meal together to discuss the project, work methods and progress. Quality was a hallmark of the guilds. Master craftsmen signed their work with the guild seal or symbol. By contrast, the Industrial Revolution reconstituted the way work was done in much of the Western world, including America. Its enduring contribution was to bring the benefits of increased *quantity* to manufacturing and processing tasks. Quality standards took a secondary role.

The early impetus of the Scientific Management movement was initially on quality. But quantity factors soon predominated and reduced the focus on individual and unit quality. Nevertheless, early scientific managers introduced technologies like time and motion study, statistical quality control and reliance on jigs, standard patterns and similar techniques to focus worker and managers alike on quality performance.

In the last decades of the twentieth century, America has evolved from an industrial society to an information society (Naisbitt and Aburdene, 1985). Naisbitt and Aburdene suggest that the human resource is more valuable in today's work world than money was in the industrial age. If America has a competitive advantage it is in its people. The American work force traditionally has been committed, motivated and prepared educationally and psychologically to produce at high performance levels.

The pressure is intense to provide more and more things to a growing and demanding population. This pressure to produce has minimized the independent craftsman's role. As a result, much of the responsibility to secure high quality is built into corporate structures and systems and may not depend on the attitudes and values of the organization's people. Today we delegate the problem of increasing quality to third parties, who examine workers' products after the fact. Now inspectors, behavior modification experts (who often use implied threats or bribes to induce workers to produce at predetermined levels) and quality control units have responsibility for quality. The results have been to continue to increase quantity, but at the expense of quality.

The 1970s and 1980s especially brought a renewed interest in making quality a value in contemporary American business and government cultures. Spurred by the successful application of quality control techniques coupled with participative structures in Japan after World War II, some American organizations moved into this technology. Current systems typically focus on a commitment to organization-wide quality, customer service and measurement of performance effort.

The quality movement also impacted leadership theory. It gave rise to the excellence movement most prevalent in the 1980s and is still a minor thread in leadership theory.

THE MODERN QUALITY FOCUS

The origins of the most recent ideas about leadership as a focus on excellence stem from the work of Peters and Waterman (1982). Their book, *In Search of Excellence*, relates excellence to caring for others, innovation and high-quality service, with innovation being the key factor. But it is innovation in an environment of honest concern for all stakeholders.

For Peters and Austin (1985) leadership connotes the task of unleashing follower energy, building, freeing and allowing for their growth. Their definition recasts the dedicated, analytical manager as an enthusiastic coach. Excellent leaders strengthen followers and recognize in tangible ways their creative contributions. This recognition allows followers to grow and the corporation to prosper.

To foster excellence in followers, leaders need to allow them some control in their work and to let them know what the whole organization is all about. Excellent leaders create a culture that fosters excellence. Excellent corporations develop cultures that incorporate the values and practices of excellent leaders. Excellent leaders instill a sense of vision of the potential of the individual and the corporation.

PRINCIPLES OF LEADERSHIP EXCELLENCE

Excellence cultures are decentralized. They devolve responsibility on the work force (e.g., through Quality Circles or self-directed work teams). This is an emphasis on inspiring leadership as opposed to management based on refined skills. This kind of culture is committed to development and concern for workers. It is results-oriented, not merely activity-oriented. This model of leadership is concerned with behaviors that link performance expectations to such compensations as motivation, inspiration, commitment to doing right things, pride in accomplishments, ethics, participation and trust.

At least five aspects of a definition can be abstracted from the literature. In order of priority, they are

A Focus on Quality

The excellence leader's job is to encourage and sustain high-quality products and service to all who have a stake in the group's work. Excellence leadership incorporates ideas that energize and inspire followers to unified action to increase and maintain high-quality services and products. These leaders focus on high-quality performance in all aspects of work. They foster team approaches to task activity that delegate more discretion over the work to the team and to individuals. They set standards of conduct and performance that implement cultural values and behaviors. This leadership model includes encouraging the formation of traditions that foster and inculcate the core-value vision. Often it includes dramatizing the core-value vision in ways that explain and interpret it to organization members.

This virtual leadership environment assumes a culture of excellence. Culture includes experience, expectation for the future and values that condition behavior. Without general agreement on acceptable behavior and the values context within which we operate, corporation members are free to follow divergent paths. Coherent, cooperative action is impossible where at least implicit agreement in a common culture is missing. Creating and maintaining a culture conducive to attainment of personal and team excellence goals is, therefore, a hallmark of this kind of leadership.

A Focus on Vision

The principal mechanism for implementing values and purposes the leader desires is the vision statement. A vision statement is a short, memorable motto or statement that encapsulates the core values of the organization. Creating the statement is a personal task done primarily by the leader. The excellent leader adopts a core-value vision that emphasizes quality improvement values.

The impact of vision setting is powerful. It pervades all else the excellent leader does. It is both part of the definition of the excellent leader and the mechanism for integrating context (culture) and technologies. It is the core idea binding leader and followers in a common purpose.

A Focus on Service

Also critical is the need for the leader to address questions of high-quality service in attaining corporate goals. In doing this, leaders act to prepare and then empower followers to be of service. This aspect of the service dimension is similar to the training and education programs managers and leaders have been doing routinely. If there is a difference in these activities associated with excellence leadership, it is in the effort to prepare the follower to be of service on a wider front. Excellence leaders see value in helping followers broadly develop their capacity to be of service. They also emphasize high-quality, excellent service levels.

The second aspect of the service dimension has to do with the service role of the leader toward followers. The leader's job is not only to encourage and sustain high-quality service by all stakeholders but to provide needed services to all those who have a stake in the group's work. Leaders serve coworkers as their needs arise so they (the followers) can accomplish their set tasks.

Leaders serve followers in ways that energize and inspire them to unified action. The service role casts the leader as a steward in relationships with coworkers. The stewardship role asks the leader to hold in trust the organization, its resources, its people and the common vision of the future.

A Focus on Innovation

Leaders foster innovation in the group. The excellence leadership model sees the leader's role as transforming the self, followers and the institution to achieve the strategic vision. Leaders see their role as transforming the group. Excellence leaders have a bias for change. They are alert to the expressed and implied needs of customers, employees and clients. They respect both the techniques and the pressures for change.

Leaders develop their followers in appropriate ways to enhance them and improve their performance. Leaders love people. They expend large amounts of energy in seeking, developing and expanding the capacities of those around them. Excellence leadership is in the business of making champions. Champions are group members imbued with the leader's vision and capable of moving an idea through all the development phases to full implementation.

A Focus on Productivity Improvement

Productivity improvement is also part of the definition of the excellence leader. Excellence leaders take responsibility for improvement in the productive capacity of the group and its members. These leaders have a results-oriented, not activity-oriented, service style. There is an uncompromising commitment to the customer. They inspire others to think, plan and act with the customer's need in mind (Reuss, 1987).

Productivity, therefore, becomes a function of directed service. Excellence leaders encourage productivity through reward structures contingent upon the demonstration of desired productivity behaviors (Bass, Waldman and Avolio, 1987). Excellence leadership focuses the leader on reward structures that encourage high-quality work. Leaders provide incentives for stakeholders to change to accommodate the vision values. Rewards in excellence leadership emphasize development of individual capacities and respect for group values, norms, work processes and productivity results.

4

Defining Quality Operationally

The dictionary definition of quality includes ideas of excellence. George Edwards defines it as existing when successive articles of commerce have their characteristics more nearly like their fellows and more nearly approximating the designer's intent (in Lammermeyer, 1990). Crosby (1984) defines quality as conforming to requirements. He says we attain quality best by having everyone do it right the first time. Joseph M. Juran (1989) defines quality as freedom from waste, trouble and failure. Others suggest that quality is meeting and exceeding informed customer needs.

Others define quality in global terms. They suggest it is a composite of the characteristics of all corporate components, such as design, engineering, manufacture, marketing and maintenance, that a given product and service receives. Defined in this way, quality is a function of any work activity, including seeking customer satisfaction. Today many people place a strong emphasis on customer satisfaction, not engineering, in defining quality. They see quality as a way of managing, not a task of management.

W. Edwards Deming (1986) was a founder of the so-called Third Wave of the Industrial Revolution. He also defines quality in customer satisfaction terms. Quality is the result of forecasting customer needs and translating them into product characteristics to create useful and dependable products. Quality is, in effect, creating a system that can deliver the product at the lowest possible price consistent with both customers' and producers' needs. Deming produced a philosophy of quality consisting of fourteen points that defines quality enhancement as more than a system of techniques.

Samuelson (1984) suggests that excellence is not simply thinking that all so-called excellent organizations are worker utopias. We haven't yet found a formula for universal worker satisfaction. However, some factors are helpful. A key to excellence leadership is to surround the leader with excellent people. To do this, leaders need to understand their followers' capacities and their corporation's particular niche in society. Leaders must also be willing to sometimes innovate solutions in critical situations (Flom, 1987).

Excellence leaders foster cultures that include reward systems that favor top performers. In addition, in this leadership reality there is an emphasis on values of excellence, quality service and innovation and caring for stakeholders. Excellence cultures are decentralized. They devolve responsibility on the work force. They employ techniques such as Quality Circles or worker's councils. Excellent leaders are committed to developing and cherishing the work force. They develop work systems that incorporate both productivity and caring values.

The organizational surround helps foster these kinds of people values. The culture encourages and rewards effective leadership throughout the organization. It fosters program or task champions. A central feature of this kind of culture is close interaction between leaders, workers and customers at all levels. These corporate systems and values emphasize concern with process, rather than product, and with people over either product or process (Porter, Sargent and Stupack, 1987). Such a culture focuses on one service or product system as opposed to multi-differentiated service systems.

DOING QUALITY WORK

Where once quality was only one element among many in corporate management, in this virtual environment it is the key element. The firm's effectiveness in quality terms is more a function of the attitudes and style of the leader and the culture he or she creates than a function of a specific managerial control system. Quality is not so much insuring that systems of work include an inspection component, as it is a part of the values, purposes and goals of both leaders and followers. It is a part of the value system of corporate leaders and other stakeholders, not a separate add-on system.

The current total quality management (TQM) fad is a comprehensive example of current quality enhancement programs. Under TQM the total work process by which we produce and distribute products and services to customers is the focus of improvement. TQM experts see work process as the amalgam of workers, material, equipment, customers, suppliers and all other stakeholders, as well as the larger community within which the firm is housed. The task of TQM is the continuous improvement of this comprehensive work system. The way to do this is to insure the integration of workers and processes in the most efficient way to produce a continually improving production process.

Most customers expect only what corporate leaders have led them to expect. In TQM the leader's job is to teach both workers and customers—indeed, all stakeholders—what they need in the way of quality products and to value high-quality products or services. A wise customer will listen and learn from a supplier.

TQM technologies are a routine part of the leader's activity on the job. Leaders also use some other techniques, albeit more rarely. Leaders consciously engage in activities to insure that all coworkers uniformly accept and value corporate goals and methods. They occasionally sponsor individuals in innovative activities that may risk agency resources. And sometimes they form groups and councils to consider quality improvement changes or other improvements.

Leaders also use many of the other common leadership techniques discussed in the literature. Thus, they sometimes engage in activities designed to inspire coworkers to higher performance. They do this by manipulating scarce resources, recognizing outstanding performance, setting organizational values and otherwise establishing expectations of excellence. While these and other behaviors noted are present, they represent an underuse of available excellence leadership technologies. They are targets of opportunity for the future in helping employees make fuller use of their capacities in vision-directed activity.

In the following sections we describe some specific presently used quality improvement systems in terms of their salient elements. Their success is a function of the capacity to induce stakeholders to accept the values underlying quality enhancement, not just the discrete tools or systems to control worker performance. In this sense, quality is a factor in culture management rather than in task control or supervision.

Methods to Improve Quality Performance

Prioritizing Quality Service

The thought processes of leadership excellence focus leaders' attention and group energy on quality service. The intent is to change coworkers so they internalize the quality value in performing their work. Leaders are involved in creating and maintaining work systems that emphasize results, measurement of quality and implementation performance (Danforth, 1987). The search for quality extends to hiring, training, placement and inspiration of coworkers.

The quest for quality asks corporation members to accept the quality value and act in accordance with this standard. Attaining quality performance today requires the concerted effort of all levels in the organization. The first step is to recognize that a quality improvement process can be of benefit to both the corporation and individual members. Other steps involve specific training in improved techniques and institution of measurement systems to evaluate progress.

Celebrations

Celebration is the excellence technique of taking time to reinforce desired behavior or results and to acknowledge a job well done. It is a pause to acknowledge corporate and individual success. Celebrations bind followers to a common cause. Celebrations recognize both group and individual performance. They dramatize the leader's commitment to corporate excellence goals and acceptance of that challenge by individual workers.

Celebrations can take place at any time. Often they mark the end of a period of hard work on a project. They are rewards. Excellent leaders reward their employees (in celebrations that deliver the best regards of top management), when groups or individuals meet established standards of conduct or results. Celebrations are also held when individuals or groups demonstrate exemplary behavior in creativity, imagination, foresight or other quality-oriented effort. They mark employee activity in going beyond the call of duty. Rewards given at these celebrations are often simple and fun and are related to the actual interests of the people involved.

Quality Circles

One way to get improved quality performance is to give workers prime responsibility for a mechanism to attain high quality. Quality Circles (QCs) were the managerial fad of choice in the 1980s to accomplish this. Quality Circles are small groups of about ten people, including a supervisor. They meet regularly to identify, analyze and solve problems experienced on the job.

The secret of the success of many QC programs is in the change of the virtual environment of the members of the circles (teams). Quality Circles reshape the attitudes of the people who actually do the organization's work. They become a small in-house consultant team tasked to improve conditions and results. In effect, a QC program makes the members mini-leaders, each with the same goal of improving current performance. Typically, QC teams make suggestions on how to enhance the quality of goods or services, solve workplace problems and improve corporate communications. They also implement agreed-upon suggestions. These are all tasks normally assigned to managers and leaders.

The success of QCs is a function of the members' willingness to accept and act on the responsibility to change and improve the organization. They take personal ownership of their part of the organization. Quality Circles help improve productivity. They improve employee morale. They improve interpersonal problem-solving skills. They can improve the level of service to customers. These are all functions and goals sought by leaders.

Quality Circle programs are more a philosophy of worker self-governance than just a program of action. To be effective the QC must be an integral part of the organization's management philosophy. Circle programs aim at improving productivity by changing the way people work together, what they value and their processes of interaction for problem solving and goal accomplishment. They ask us to treat employees as adults, trust them, respect them and help them become their best selves. This quality program asks leaders to be obsessed with quality. It requires all group members to be involved in the quest for quality (Peters, 1987).

Total Quality Management

TQM implies something other than zero defects. Traditional definitions of quality (such as automation, computerization, best efforts, more inspection, zero defects, management by objective [MBO] and quality managers) ignore the responsibility of leaders and place responsibility on workers or equipment or suppliers. Quality is the responsibility of the leaders of the company working with customers. Top management, leaders, make quality. It is determined, shaped and given meaning at the top. Workers then implement it.

TQM proposes that our best efforts must be guided by knowledge developed by leaders, not customers. Contrary to popular myth, corporate customers do not often provide useful information about what they need and the level of quality required. Often customers do not know what is possible or what options may be open to them respecting new or higher-quality products or services. Leaders do! They create most of today's new products and services and then sell it to their customers. Beyond doubt, this is the case with computer software houses. It is also the case for most innovations in automobile manufacture and other service and consumer product industries. The manufacturers and suppliers develop new products and then induce customers to see their value.

DEMING'S MANAGEMENT PHILOSOPHY

Mention has been made of the contributions of W. Edwards Deming to the development of a culture of quality enhancement in leadership. He summarizes his philosophy in his now famous Fourteen Points. Each of these fourteen principles helps define the process of quality creation. His principles speak to the need to create constancy of purpose toward improvement of products and services. They guide leaders in adopting a philosophy of quality and rejecting the idea that the work group can accept delays, mistakes, defective materials or faulty workmanship.

Deming (1986) suggests that business organizations end the practice of awarding business based on component price alone. He assigns managers the task of continually working to improve the system, institute modern methods of training and employ different methods to supervise of workers. He says the responsibility of the foreman must change from numbers to quality.

Deming's program goals include the elimination of fear so everyone may work effectively for the company. Leaders break down the barriers between departments. They abolish numerical goals and slogans for the work force, asking instead for new levels of productivity without providing detailed methods that employees can better supply. The intent of the Deming philosophy is to remove the barriers that stand between workers and their right to pride of workmanship.

Deming's Fourteen Points guide excellence leaders along the range of quality improvement tasks. For example, he asks leaders to begin to require constancy of purpose, including developing and promoting a long-term corporate commitment to changing the workplace to make it better. He suggests they adopt the philosophy that we can no longer deal with the commonly accepted levels of delays, mistakes, defective materials and defective workmanship.

Deming advised leaders that excellence cannot come when we continue to set specific numerical goals. Abolishing numerical goals lets us focus on improving the process of work, not just its results. The leader's job is to continually work on improving the system. It is to create a management structure that will push every day for high quality.

Deming says excellence leaders should inaugurate modern methods of leadership of workers. The responsibility of leaders—from foremen to top management—must change from numbers to quality. One way to do this is to drive out fear from the work place. Leaders should take the fear out of bad news, so all workers can use the information to improve the processes and strive for the lowest product price.

Leaders, Deming said, break down departmental barriers. They unite all units in corporate mission accomplishment and quality improvement, mostly through individual training on the job. A vigorous program of education and self-development training fosters teamwork. As leaders foster the employees' pride in their work, quality improves. Personal pride, not traditional programs of annual merit rating, raises quality. Merit rating is unfair and harmful. To measure individual performance fosters jealousy and destructive competition.

Deming also advocated the elimination of slogans and exhortations. They foster an adversarial relationship since employees alone cannot change the organization; nor can dependence on mass inspection. Rather, he said, leaders should design processes that identify faults early and prevent production of defective materials.

Deming's principles ask managers to become leaders. That is, they ask them to manage values, change attitudes and establish a new vision (Deming called it an aim). This vision is that continuous improvement in the system is desirable, possible and the central task of the leader. In every essential respect, Deming's philosophy is a prescription for corporate change, for a new virtual environment emphasizing excellence.

JURAN'S QUALITY PHILOSOPHY

Another pioneer in the quality movement is Joseph M. Juran. Juran was chief of the inspection control division of Western Electric Company and a professor at New York University. He taught a ten-step method for implementing quality that is similar to Deming's Fourteen Points. Juran's philosophy centers on building awareness of the need and opportunity for improvement. He suggests that leaders set goals for improvement and organize to reach these goals. Juran supports establishment of quality councils to identify problems, select projects, appoint teams and choose facilitators.

His quality councils represent a new form of corporate structure based on values of quality, sharing and participation. They provide training in quality techniques to workers who then carry out projects to solve problems. His approach includes elements of accountability through regular progress reporting.

Other elements of his philosophy involve giving recognition for quality performance, broadly communicating quality enhancement skills developed by one council and keeping score—that is, routinely recording progress to insure that all workers know and understand the organization's priority on quality performance. The bottom line of the Juran philosophy is making improvement part of the regular values, work systems and processes of the company.

5

Skills Needed for Leadership Excellence

Leadership excellence appears to be an applied capacity. It is action-oriented, and it cannot be learned in classrooms. Of course, some leadership skills are acquired in the normal way through reading, studying and analyzing theoretical propositions and principles. And some leadership capacity is learned through observation of other leaders. But leadership excellence is learned most fully through leadership action. It is a dynamic process. One study of executives in Virginia (Fairholm, 1991) identified eight categories of skills that seem to define the technology of excellence. They include

- Ability to assess the situation
- Capacity to build on employee strengths
- Sensitivity to evolving trends
- Political astuteness
- Refined sense of timing
- Capacity to be inspirational
- Technical (job) competence
- Ability to focus on a few important things

The factors that promote excellence in organizations across the nation include clarity of mission and vision and effective leadership at the top. Excellence leaders select and support service champions (in-house entrepreneurs). They interact closely with both employees and customers. They understand cultures and structures, emphasize process over product and focus on human factors to get a high-quality product.

These skills run counter to much of the content of professional business school curricula. These schools teach quantitative analysis and rational decision making as primary technologies. Evidence amassed in leadership excellence suggests otherwise. Unlike management, leadership excellence is more a political process of defining the situation, assessing the strengths of actors, sensing nuances in relationships and acting to focus group resources at the right time. Technical competence in the job to be done is less important than political sensitivity.

Preparation for leadership excellence asks embryonic leaders to be political, to be sensitive to the feelings of others and to care about their followers as human beings, not as just cogs in the industrial machine. Leaders who focus too much on traditional managerial goals of tight control will fall short of attainable high-quality performance and can expect failure, even destruction. Quality improvement is a long-term values-change process. There are few quick successes.

Attaining high quality requires total employee involvement at all levels in the organization. It is a matter of cultural change to give high priority to quality values and methods. It requires effort by everyone: workers, middle managers and those at the top. Each needs to play a role in changing the culture to value quality and in performing to attain it.

Producing high-quality products or services also implies quality-of-work-life factors that are difficult to attain. Excellence leaders need to create a culture that meets the needs of all stakeholders both within and external to the organization. They need to give employees something personally meaningful to commit to before they commit themselves to quality goals or anything else (Pascerella, 1984). Ludeman (1989) suggests, rightly, that we need to replace the old Protestant work ethic with a "worth ethic."

High quality will come only as we move from a situation where workers work because they fear economic deprivation, to a situation where they work because they want to improve themselves and make a difference in the world. It is an empowerment idea.

PERSONAL LEADER ACTION TECHNOLOGIES

The sense of the literature describing the virtual environment of leadership excellence is on three kinds of technologies, three sets of techniques, methods, behaviors and attitudes. One excellence technology impacts directly on the leader as an individual, on his or her behavior and leadership style. A second technology is directed outward from the leader to his or her followers. These methods and attitudes deal with helping clients and employees change. Indeed, leadership excellence deals with both the leader and all stakeholders. The third technology deals with the organizational environmental situation within which leadership excellence takes place.

Perhaps the most critical feature of the leadership excellence model is the behavior exhibited by individual leaders. As they incorporate excellence principles into their lives, they change. As the leader's behavior toward others changes, the organization changes. The techniques of leadership change are many and varied. They all center on an overriding concern for the development of others so that both the leader and the followers can do a better job in doing the organization's work. We can list at least four specific techniques that are identified in the literature as unique to leadership excellence.

The most significant characteristics of this behavior are summed up in the idea that leaders care for and respect their stakeholders. This caring behavior is demonstrated in courtesy, listening to understand and otherwise showing respect for and acceptance of the ideas, actions and opinions of coworkers and other stakeholders. These leaders have a penchant for close interaction with coworkers.

In the years that the leadership excellence model has been operational (roughly 1980 to the present, but concentrating in the 1980s) several techniques have been developed. They focus on the skills and attitudes leaders need to be successful. These skills and attributes have come to epitomize the excellence-oriented leader. They help define and delimit both the model and the range of acceptable leader behavior. These patterned techniques make up the technology of the excellence leader. The four techniques are common courtesy; management by wandering around; showing caring behavior; and paying attention to critical values, actions and goals needed to reach vision outcomes.

Common Courtesy

Deceptively simple, showing courtesy to others works. A central idea is that leaders can increase quality commitment in their employees through the simple act of being courteous in their relationships with them. We all respond well to respectful and kind behavior. Excellence leaders respect the talent, feelings and concerns of workers and other stakeholders including customers. This sometimes uncommon behavior works, but only if the relationship is authentic.

Management by Wandering Around

Excellence leadership is done by wandering around in all of the corporation's workstations (Peters and Waterman, 1982). It puts leaders in touch (literally) with workers and their work and with customers and their concerns. It balances book knowledge about the corporation with working knowledge of the work being done. Wandering around means getting out of the office and experiencing firsthand how the corporation is operating and what the problems of workers are.

Excellence leaders cultivate people critical to their success and all other stakeholders, including ordinary workers. Wandering around is a name for an extensive network of informal, open communications with all stakeholders. The purpose is to tap information sources and gain a mutual understanding of what is going on, what is needed and how to go about closing the gap between them. It involves staying in regular, informal contact with coworkers and other stakeholders at *their* work sites, not just in formal conference rooms.

Caring Behavior

Excellence leaders respect their people. They expend large amounts of time and other resources in seeking, developing and expanding the capacities of those around them who are similarly engaged in the common work. Barbour, Fletcher and Sipel (1984) contend that leadership excellence involves a highly developed concern for employees and the firm as an institution. Real craftsmanship, regardless of the skill involved, reflects authentic caring, and real caring reflects our attitudes about ourselves, our fellows and life itself. Leadership excellence reflects this kind of caring,which is similar to the feeling craftsmen have about their craft.

Paying Attention

Leadership excellence is about caring about people, but this is not enough. Excellent leaders also pay attention to quality services, to innovation, to a guiding vision, to enthusiasm for the common work, to pride and passion. Leadership excellence is primarily a task of focusing and paying attention to what the leader feels is important.

We all pay attention to something. The problem is to select and consistently focus on what the corporation needs and wants. Paying attention is focusing on one thing as opposed to all other things. Focusing helps the leader communicate a consistent message to followers and all stakeholders and to the larger communities within which the corporation exists. Focusing tells members of the group and the world what the leader thinks is important.

In summary, the literature of leadership excellence describes a new kind of leader, one markedly different from the traditional managerial model. It is not so much that the old model is wrong, just incomplete.

While it specified elements of style, the style it espoused was sterile. While it included elements of interpersonal relationships, the relationships defined lacked passion, emotion and commitment. The managerial virtual environment is founded on one value: efficiency. The leadership excellence model is supported by values that promote the development of others, in addition to efficiency.

While past leadership theory may have been limiting, past practice has not. The practice of leadership is and always has been active, dynamic and personal. The essence of leadership coming out of this mental environment is in the relationships created more than the structural systems produced. Excellence values honor people, innovation and high-quality service. The leader's ability to inculcate these ideals and demonstrate them in his or her relationships with stakeholders and in the corporate culture is the measure of success. As leaders prepare themselves to lead on the basis of excellence, they must emphasize development, service, self-direction and intimacy in their work with employees and all stakeholders.

LEADER ACTION TECHNOLOGIES DIRECTED TOWARD STAKEHOLDERS

Preparation is important, but success comes only as leaders interact with followers. The critical relationships are not with self, but with employees as the leader tries to get them to want to perform excellently. Two technologies among several that might be identified in this connection are crucial: coaching and empowerment. These technologies are reflective of the techniques that excellence research says enhances followers.

Coaching

Coaching is a teaching technology. It involves the ongoing support excellence leaders give followers to help them prepare themselves to act on behalf of the corporation. Coaching is a new conception of the leader's role. Few writers prior to the 1980s related leadership to teaching. Henry Levinson (1968) is the exception. Coaching means acting in ways that enable others to act independently. It is face-to-face leadership. Its purpose is to bring out the best in individuals, to build on their strengths. At its heart, coaching involves caring enough about people to take the time to build personal relationships with them. It is the power of personal attention that can be communicated in only one way: personal presence.

Empowerment

The virtual environment of traditional management viewed employees, at best, as parts of the corporate machine: interchangeable and anonymous. While they may have been important to success, employees were essentially viewed as bundles of skills, knowledge and abilities that were useful to the manager in the production process. Other employee capacities than those needed to do a specific set of tasks were ignored and were often even viewed as detrimental to full success.

Times have changed. People have changed. Workers will no longer accept this limited view of themselves and their level of contribution to the collective enterprise. Workers today are better educated and far more independent than they formerly were. Workers are more aware of what is possible for them, and therefore they want more. Pfeffer (1977) says that people want to achieve feelings of control over their environment.

People want to make a difference, and the leader will gain followers if he or she allows or teaches them how to do this. Conger and Kanungo (1988) define empowerment in terms of motivation. For them, it is enabling, rather than simply delegation. Bennis and Nanus (1985) says it is helping people feel significant. It is aiding them in learning, involving them in the group and making the work exciting for them. Empowered people respond to work and to crises at work with commitment; powerless people do not.

Empowering others is pulling them, not pushing them; it is translating intention into action and sustaining it. It is moving people from believing to doing to becoming. Being empowered enlarges the perception of employees and gets them to explore possibilities. It raises their ability to perform. It releases the power in others through collaboration. It endows employees with the power required to perform a given act, and it grants them the practical autonomy to step out and contribute directly—in their unique ways—to the job.

LEADER ACTIONS TO CHANGE THE ORGANIZATIONAL SURROUND

Excellence leaders also work to change corporate culture to value quality. Four factors impact the character of the excellence corporate culture: culture settin, strategic planning, standard setting and vision setting. These factors are important aspects of the actions excellence leaders take to alter the environment to make the firm more accepting of excellence activity.

Culture Setting

Culture exists at the symbolic level of human existence. Organizational culture is not so much an official position of values promulgated by management as it is a whole range of shared models of social action containing both real and ideal elements. Culture is the invisible quality—a certain style, a character, a way of doing things that may be more powerful than the dictates of any one person or any formal system. Life experiences, historical traditions, class positions and political circumstances shape cultures. All of these are powerful forces that resist directed change (Reynolds, 1986).

Culture is dependent on the actions of leaders. Their objectives, visions, values and (importantly) behavior provide clues as to what is really expected and accepted. Culture management may be the most essential activity leaders engage in in seeking excellence.

Strategic Planning

Strategy involves trying to understand where you sit in today's world. It is quite different from plan implementation. It is akin to vision setting (Brassier, 1985). Thus, strategy development and strategic systems are central activities of excellence leaders. The purpose is to integrate corporate units and enable the headquarters to capitalize on synergies. Managers in all kinds of organizations use strategic planning techniques to identify critical issues that face their organizations. Strategic plans operationalize the vision and define what they want the corporation to be in the future. Strategies can be a primary source of cohesiveness in the organization (Eadie, 1983).

Standard Setting

Standards are measures of quality that are used to push performance toward vision outcomes. As such, they have been a part of management from the beginning. What is innovative about standard setting in the leader-as-good-manager virtual environment, is the relating of standards to the leader's vision. Excellence leadership is, in part, generalizing quality standards so that all concerned understand them, live them and encourage others to live them. Setting quality standards helps leaders keep the non-essential from getting in the way of what is important.

Vision Setting

Visioning is more than goal setting. It involves activating the emotions as well as the mind. Visioning has a strong value connotation; it is more than rational. It involves the leader in setting a future vision for the group, promoting that vision and planning strategically to attain it. Visioning is a characteristic of excellence leaders. The vision statement is a primary tool for explaining ourselves to our bosses—higher management, clients, customers, citizens. The leader's vision carries the powerful message that the future is vital and will be different. We cannot predict it, but we can create it (Brassier, 1985).

Leading based on excellence goals involves the leader in setting and articulating a vision of the organization that focuses on improvement of quality. Establishing an excellence culture, strategies for action and quality standards are important, but group members need more. They need a central guiding purpose toward which they can bend their mutual efforts. Visioning is analogous to setting the superordinate goals that Pascale and Athos (1981) discussed or that Bradford and Cohen (1984) called overarching goal setting. It is, at heart, a challenging, unifying, unique and creditable statement of what the corporation is and can become.

SUMMARY AND CONCLUSIONS

Leadership excellence is partly about transforming the leader's virtual environment, partly about changing the perceptions of followers and partly about transforming the common culture. Excellence is not attained in the absence of a congruence of all of these factors. In the attainment of these results, all three are improved, developed, matured. Leadership excellence is a change process affecting all stakeholders and the institution itself.

This leadership mind-set changes each group member into something more than they were before. This transformation takes place in a consciously created and managed culture that prioritizes quality excellence. The leader-as-excellent-manager virtual environment provides the root structure supporting the leadership tree that now is defined in terms of values, culture and the spiritual center of both leader and led.

PART III

Values Leadership

Expanding past management models only complicates the process of creating a viable virtual environment appropriate to today's tasks. Fortunately, there is a new way to view leadership on the horizon. This new virtual environment defines the leader's purpose as helping individuals become proactive contributors to group action. It is values-based, future-change-oriented and seeks to develop people. Our past reluctance to deal directly with the foundaiton of values to leadership in our social groups ignores a vital element of our understanding and limits our collective capacity to lead.

A central feature of leadership philosophy is its emphasis on a few values held in common by group members. These values are summarized in a vision of what the group and its members are and can become. In the United States, the vision typically integrates values described first by the founding fathers. These values include personal liberty, respect for life, justice, unity and happiness. These are common values that are intrinsically held and to the realization of which most people devote their energies. Unless leaders tap these energizing values, they risk not being able to lead.

6

Overview of Past Leadership Theories

Leadership is the preeminent need in society's institutions. As America and the world enter a new century, their institutions are undergoing fundamental pressures to adapt. The world is becoming one community. Complex global demands for change are affecting local organizations. These worldwide pressures are making past points of view, methods, ideas and models of leadership obsolete.

Workers are becoming more educated, more demanding and more articulate in voicing their needs. They are asking to participate and share in both the results of their labor and the methods they use. And, importantly, our customers are becoming more involved in the day-to-day work of the corporation. They are demanding direct involvement in shaping corporate policies and even work systems that deliver the services they require.

Past leadership virtual environments just don't work in this changed world. They confuse the careful observer by inappropriately linking leadership with management. They focus on skills, structure and system concepts that are firmly within the realm of management, not leadership. Leadership is more than technical skill in analysis, exercising control and organizing (Merget, 1989). It deals with people, their development and growth, and fosters loyalty and commitment to group values and results. At their worst, the past management-oriented virtual environments divert our thinking from real leadership principles. At best they are only precursors of the values-leadership virtual environment described below. Past theories contain parts of the guiding values and behaviors central to true leadership, but not its essential whole.

Values leadership is coming to be a name descriptive of a special way to think about the role and functions of leadership. Its principles define the parameters of thought, values, actions and results more than they define particular structures and relationships systems. Values leadership is a way to think about leadership founded in individual and corporate values. It emphasizes the individual in the group, not just the organization. Individual, not corporate, values predominate.

Over the years, answers to the question, "What makes a good leader?" have resulted in several theoretical orientations, each strongly advocated in its day. All are still somewhat helpful. Some define leadership in managerial terms, others in personal terms, and still others in situational terms. Holding a high-status position does not make one a leader. Some high office holders are chief managers or head custodians or mere figureheads. High status, however, is not irrelevant to leadership. There are positions that carry with them symbolic values and traditions that enhance the possibilities of leadership. An obvious example is the President of the United States of America. Of course, position alone does not make the leader; nor does the capacity to impose rewards or punishments define the leader. Consequences are not a reliable measure of leadership; relationships are. Management connotes controlling; leadership connotes unleashing the energy of followers. Leadership is building followers, freeing them and allowing them to grow (Peters and Austin, 1985).

THEORIES OF WHO THE LEADER *IS*

Three generic leadership environments are clear in past theory. As we analyze the many leadership theories (taken from management theory building), we can classify them into one of three virtual environments. Some concern who the leader *is*, others focus on what the leader *does*, and some deal with where leadership *takes place*. A brief review of each virtual environment may help place what follows in perspective.

The first leadership mental environment dealt with the person of the leader: his or her traits, capacities and individual talents. An initial perspective, it focused on people who occupied significant positions and impacted societies in important ways. Theorists assumed these people possessed a personality naturally inclined toward leadership. This so-called Great Man model proposed that individuals take leadership because they are born with superior qualities that differentiate them from others. Identifying these qualities would make it possible to recognize emergent leaders or to discipline those qualities to improve existing leaders.

More popular today, trait theory argues that common traits, if identifiable in recognized leaders, would help others develop their leadership capacities. Early studies identified such characteristics as social sensitivity, masculinity, personal appearance and moodiness. However, these studies did not isolate a single trait or group of traits that set the leader off from others. Indeed, Charles Bird (1940) examined 20 lists of so-called leader traits. He found that not one item ostensibly related to leadership appeared on all 20 lists.

Leadership has also occupied the attention of psychologists, who see leaders as father figures and therefore as sources of love, the embodiment of fear or the embodiment of the superego. Psychological approaches are implicit in most leadership theory and explicit in some. These approaches define leaders through analysis of their childhood deprivations, cultural experiences, parental relations and the needs they fulfill for followers.

Theories of who the leader is help us understand one important aspect of leadership—the character of the individual leader. They do not do much to predict future leaders or anticipate leader behavior. They are of even less help in leadership development. New, more operationally specific, theories were needed. One such theory looked to personal traits and behavior in combination.

THEORIES OF WHAT THE LEADER *DOES*

Difficulty in isolating universal leader traits led to a behavioral focus. Behavioral leadership theory has attracted much attention since the middle part of the twentieth century. The rationale is that concentrating on studying observable behavior may be more operationally useful than looking at traits.

Tannenbaum and Schmidt (1973) see leader behavior as a continuum from manager-centered to subordinate-centered behavior. They proposed that defining leadership behavior was a means to change follower behavior. Davis and Luthans (1979) concluded that leaders do not cause follower behavior. Leaders merely set the occasion or provide a stimulus for the evocation of follower behavior. Behavior, for them, represented environmental cues, discriminative stimuli and results of behaviors that form a behavioral contingency for action.

Rensis Likert (1961), of the Michigan State University leadership research group, defined four basic behavior patterns of leaders. His model follows McGregor's (1960) Theory X and Theory Y assumptions—from highly job-centered to highly people-centered.

Blake and Mouton (1964) [from the Ohio State leadership research group] found a different result from their research. They concluded that, while initiating structure and idea development are discrete orientations in theory, persons in life show some of each characteristic.

Interaction-expectancy theories emphasize the expectancy factor in the leader-follower relationship. Homans (1956) developed a leadership role theory of three variables: action, interactions and sentiments. Leaders act to initiate structure-facilitating interactions, and leadership is the act of initiating such structures. Stogdill (1957) developed an expectancy-reinforcement theory that defines the leader's role as setting mutually confirmed expectations about follower performances and interactions that followers can provide to the group.

Bass (1981) proposed a reinforced change theory. For him, the purpose of change occurring in the behavior of the group is to increase the rewards (or expectations) for desired performance. Leaders gain their positions because of their perceived abilities to reinforce the behavior of group members by granting or denying rewards and punishments.

Evens (1970) and others suggested that leaders could determine the followers' perception of the rewards available to them. The leader determines the followers' perception of the behaviors required to get needed rewards. Yukl (1981) postulated that leaders' increase follower task skills. He said leader consideration and decentralized decision making increase the motivation of subordinates. In turn, follower skill and motivation increase effectiveness.

Exchange theory compares leader-follower relationships to economic transactions. Group members contribute at a cost to them and receive returns at a cost to each group member. Interaction continues because members find social exchange mutually rewarding. Effective leadership implies a fair exchange between leader and follower, when each party can satisfy the expectations of the other on a fair basis.

Perceptual and cognitive theories focus on analysis and rational-deductive approaches to leadership. In attribution theory, leadership activity is dependent on what we think leaders should be and do. We see leader behavior and infer causes of these behaviors to be various personal traits or external constraints. We assume the causes are a function of an experience-based rational process, internalized by the leader.

Some also define leadership in systems analysis terms. The open system imports energy, power and information; changes them; and exports goods and services. The exchange process involves power, information and feedback to the system from the effect of the impacts made on the environment (Katz and Kahn, 1966). Vroom and Yetton (1973) joined some accepted facts about leadership into a rational structure. They determined that some factors are most likely to result in leader success. They concluded that leaders ought to be directive when they are confident that they know what to do and that their followers do not.

Behavioral theory in its several manifestations allows the analyst to define leadership in terms of acts. Leaders do act in certain ways, but focusing solely on behavior ignores critical factors in the situation and in the mind and heart of individual leaders that condition these actions. Other models of leadership quickly evolved that, at least, considered the leadership situation.

THEORIES OF WHERE LEADERSHIP *TAKES PLACE*

Neither trait nor behavioral models consider the environment within which leadership takes place. Situation theory concerns itself with the cluster of complex forces at work in the corporate environment, any of which may affect leader activity.

Situation theorists prioritize critical factors in the environmental situation in which individual leaders operate that impact on leader behavior. Thus, organization size, worker maturity, task complexity or a variety of other so-called critical contingencies condition leadership. According to this theory, situational factors are finite and vary according to several factors. A given leader behavior can be effective in only certain kinds of situations and not in others.

Contingency theorists suggest the criticality of discrete factors in the situation in which individual leaders operate. These factors influence leader behavior and need to be part of a theory of leadership. That is, leadership must change with the situation—or the situation must change to accommodate the kind of leadership exercised. Two versions of this theory are popular. First, path-goal theory involves a concentration on follower reactions to leader behavior. The second model, contingency theory, concerns itself with the cluster of complex forces at work in the corporation that affect leader activity. Organization size, worker maturity, task complexity or other critical contingencies affect leadership action.

Versions of situational theory, humanistic models of leadership focus on the development of effective and cohesive organizations. They see a basic tension between the individual in the group and the group. Their theories consider these so-called human factors in proposing models that accommodate both forces in the relationship. Humanistic theorists combine both behavioral and situational elements to define a created organizational surround that counters some factors that would otherwise be considered essentially antagonistic to human desires.

Humanistic theories revolve around a few ideas. First, they assume that people are, by nature, self-motivated. On the other hand, the corporation is, by nature, structured and controlled. The central theoretical problem is to devise a theory of leadership that allows for needed control, without thwarting the individual's motives. The aim of leadership is to change the corporation to provide freedom for individuals to realize their own potential for fulfillment and at the same time contribute to the firm's goals.

SHORTCOMINGS OF CURRENT MODELS

The present emphasis on leadership stems from the perceived lack of leadership in society and a general malaise in our social organizations. A variety of factors cause the problem, chief among them the clear failure of past theories of leadership. Situational and behavioral theory form the nexus of current leadership virtual environments. Both, however, are focused on close control of workers and the situation. These may be important in managing people, but many object to them as the basis for leading them.

The problem with past theories is that they fail to distinguish unique leadership tasks, skills, behaviors or thought processes from management actions. Leadership is not management. The latter deals with such things as performance, productivity and system. The manager's job is to make every person, system, activity, program and policy countable, measurable, predictable and, therefore, controllable. Many past so-called leadership theories stress this kind of control and are nothing more than theories of management. Some even use the two words interchangeably, thereby confusing the issue and making current leadership mind-sets irrelevant.

Leadership partakes of a different reality. Leaders, Selznick (1957) said, infuse the group with values. They think differently, value things differently, relate to others differently. They have different expectations for followers and seek different results from individuals and from the group than do managers. They impact stakeholder groups in a volitional way, not through formal authority mechanisms. Leadership and management are separate technologies, with different agendas, motivations, personal histories and thought processes.

Leaders don't always provide this stability. Leaders are forever innovating, moving outside the constraints of structure. While this may be exciting, it is also sometimes disconcerting. And it is hard to predict or control. On the theory (not necessarily correct) that control is more profitable than innovation, society's institutions and business corporations have moved to adopt control mechanisms that make it possible to constrain and predict the behavior of work systems, resources and people. That is, our organizations tend to move to management forms and processes and away from leadership.

Given these essential differences between leadership and management, past theories that combined the two systems of behavior and ideology must necessarily be faulty. They ignore essential features of each or else overemphasize features of one to the detriment of the other. What is needed is a new theory, one that focuses fully on leadership as a discrete technology with separate systems of behaviors, techniques and methods. Such a theory can be found in the new values-based transformational-leadership virtual environment.

7

Defining Values-based Leadership

Part of the problem many have in understanding leadership has to do with definition. For most of this century leadership was considered a part of management. At best it is defined as synonymous with "good management." At worst, it is just another skill area in which managers should demonstrate competence. Given this close association with management, it is easy to assume that good management and leadership are two sides of the same coin, that success in management makes one a leader.

This pattern of thinking is changing. Fewer and fewer experts or practitioners will now argue that leadership and management are the same, or even parts of the same thought or action processes. Now the argument is that leadership and management are different in purpose, knowledge base, required skills and goals. We distinguish leaders as more personal in their orientation to group members than managers. They are more global in their thinking. Leaders, we suggest, focus on values, expectations and context.

The leader communicates indirectly, sometimes gives overlapping and ambiguous assignments and may set employees up for strife to test loyalty or the leader's personal strength. Leaders value cooperation, not just coordination. They foster ideas of unity, equality, justice and fairness in addition to efficiency and effectiveness, the bastions of management value. Leaders affect followers who are volunteers.

Leaders think differently, value people, programs and policy differently, relate to others differently. They have different expectations for followers and seek different results from individuals and from the group. We are moving away from seeing leadership as the coordination of work in relationships bounded by structure and system. Rather, we now are coming to see leadership as a kind of socio-psychological contract in which the leader and follower cooperate voluntarily.

Both the present and past argument is that leaders are more personal in their orientation to group members, more global in their thinking and focus more on values, expectations and context, rather than the control of results and methods. They impact followers and constituent groups in a volitional way, not through formal authority mechanisms. Abraham Zaleznick (1984) sees these two functions as separate, with different agendas, motivations, personal histories and thought processes.

Obviously, leadership is not management. Management deals with such issues as performance, productivity, system, control and measurement. The stress in management is to make every system, activity, program and policy countable and, therefore, controllable. Managers tend to be impersonal (e.g., objective) and passive. They prefer security, take only calculated risks, relate to people in role terms and focus on control, accounting and accountability.

Many of the so-called leadership theories stress this kind of control. In so doing they are nothing more than theories of management. In effect, these so-called leadership theories are merely theories of management action. Managers focus on control and results. Managers give clear directions, make solitary assignments and work hard for cooperation.

THE VALUES-BASED LEADERSHIP PHILOSOPHY

Leadership based on values suggests that leadership is or can be a part of the routine actions of many people in the organization, not just the preserve of a few at the top of the organizational chart. Value-based leadership is a unique virtual environment and action sequence, the central task of which is to join leader and follower actions together through a set of common values. It has little, if anything, to do with managerial orientations. Intellectually, it may be hard to classify. Operationally, we see it in all of our organizations, at least occasionally, often continuously.

Research in the 1980s and 1990s focused on the relationships engaged in, the values that underlay those relationships and the virtual environment created by the leader. The central orientation of this research is on what leaders *think about and value*. It is a philosophical model. Values define the acceptable in society and each of its organizations. They serve as standards to guide actions and choices.

People create value systems for themselves. Organizations also develop values and present members with a value structure to which they must conform or else feel discomfort. Leaders have always known this. Leadership theorists are only now coming to recognize that everyone has values and that these values control their behavior. They are only now beginning to include values-displacement ideas in their models.

The practice of leadership requires measurement and analysis *and* unifying values. People may need to be controlled and directed, but they also must be inspired. Leadership models that ignore values—as past models did—because values "contaminate" the process fail to understand the true function of leadership.

Leadership partakes of the values and principles of life as well as operational action. Therefore, it is a question of philosophy, of the principles of reality and of human nature and conduct. The philosopher deals with analysis *and* with moral values (Burns, 1978): so do leaders. On the other hand, a theorist deals with analytical ideas and data (Hofstadter, 1955). The theorist tries to order, adjust, manipulate and examine. The theoretical mind-set relates most directly to ideas about management. We cannot see philosophical principles; they are not tangible or observable, like a production line. We cannot count, measure or control them. Yet, these philosophical principles of leadership are essential to understanding the relationships within which we live and work.

Today's world asks its chief people to understand the relationships, more than just the actions, of team members. For in truth, relationships constitute the very essence of organizations. Thus, philosophical questions are central to our understanding of leadership, of society and of its institutions. They are basic. They clarify our understanding of our world and ourselves. While often the philosophical questions are general, they are nonetheless real world concerns (Honderich and Burnyeat, 1976).

The leader's task is to integrate behavior with values. If we are to improve our organizations, leaders must consider the character and attitudes they inculcate in group members, and they must model acceptable member behavior. This is, at heart, a philosophical task. It makes leadership philosophical and its operational environment value-laden and relationship-oriented.

THE ROLE OF LEADERSHIP

Management is a modern creation. Given the range and scope of recorded time, it was only recently that management skills were developed and became predominant. There is no record of the counterpart to the modern manager among the social groups and chief people of our ancient and simpler past. The great people in the ancient world were tribal chiefs, priests, generals and kings, the leaders of their times.

These chief people did not manage; they led their followers. They were in charge because they persuaded their followers that they were the strongest, the best fighters, the smartest. They controlled fire (and other resources) and wore the fanciest clothes (robes, crowns, etc.). They claimed to have the ear of the gods, receiving inspiration and visions from above. These same outward symbols of power remain. They are only changed to conform to the needs of managers and modern civilization. The transition from headship based on personality and talent to one based on control is the history of the rise of management to preeminence in our social institutions. Charismatic leadership made control over our social institutions difficult, erratic, unpredictable and unsuited to a growingly complex society. Management arose as the answer to charismatic leadership. It is headship based on persons prepared with the proper education and training.

We have come to distrust charismatic powers and have replaced them with ceremonies that can be timed, organized and controlled. Modern organizations adopted an organization and management system based on these older models. These large complex, powerful social institutions rely for success on their highly formal, tightly structured hierarchies. These formal structures constrain deviant behavior and reward compliance. While current theory and corporate cultures are moving away from this tight structure model, they were the examples used by early leadership theorists in the late nineteenth and early twentieth centuries. They remain central to much of current theory and practice.

The great leaders in art, science and literature lift their companions to new levels of beauty, craftsmanship, appreciation, understanding and skill. The qualities of leaders in all fields are the same: leaders are the ones who set the highest examples. They open the way to greater light and knowledge. They break the mold. Leaders are inspiring because they are inspired; they are caught up in a higher purpose.

Leadership places a higher emphasis on values, creativity, intelligence, integrity and sobriety. These are the traits managers seek to screen out in interviews in favor of loyalty and conformity. These qualities are needed today. Our corporations and workers cry out for interesting, exciting, challenging work and for leaders who can make the work of the world seem worth their personal time and identity.

Notwithstanding the silence of past leadership theory, these topics, these philosophical values and capacities are present in the practice of leadership. They are seen in most of our corporations. They are essential to understanding the relationships within which we work. Actually these relationships constitute the organization. Something more personal than efficient action is needed to understand how to lead business corporations.

REVIEW OF NEW VALUES-BASED LEADERSHIP THEORIES

The values-based-leadership focus deals with leader actions to create a specifically defined values context within which to practice leadership and a unique technology with definable techniques. Several writers have considered aspects of this new leadership virtual reality. Analysis of their work can clarify the underlying philosophy supporting this new leadership perspective. It helps illustrate the ways leaders apply their skills to shape group values, goals and action.

This point of view is not concerned with the leader traits of personality or behavior or with critical contingencies. This new theory focuses on the relationships engaged in, the attitudes that underlay those relationships and the philosophical "reality" adopted by the leader. Its central orientation is a philosophy of leadership—a focus on what leaders think about and value.

Peters and Waterman (1982) concluded that leaders introduce values and a culture supportive of innovation, service, quality and caring for all stakeholders. Their work is both technique- and ideology-oriented. Others have subsequently added to these ideas. Barbour and Sipel (1986) identified a leadership process that includes an emphasis on vision and that attaches meaning to work. For them, the leader's job is to develop trust in self and coworkers.

McDermott (1987) suggests that the leadership task is to create a culture focused on a shared vision of the future through collaboration. She emphasizes the values of team building, vision setting, people-oriented systems and individual development. Bradford and Cohen (1984) define a leader in terms of shared responsibility, continuous personnel development and building a common vision. They see the leader's job as changing the underlying group values to accommodate a social system characterized by multiple political relationships.

For others, the purpose of leadership is independent personal and professional growth. The employee emerges as a fully functioning human being capable of self-directed, organizationally helpful, action. Given this kind of leader-follower relationship workers see themselves as part of the larger whole with responsibility for affecting that whole.

A growing body of similar research, supports the new leadership theory, which is based on values and directed at both producing needed work effort and, importantly, developing stakeholders (Jernigan, 1997; Colvin, 1996; Martin, 1996; Fairholm, 1991, 1997). The values-based leadership principles proposed here build on this body of theory building.

These ideas ask the leader to create a vision for the corporation and then enroll members in that vision. This is a transformational leader model. Indeed, the values-based-leadership virtual environment reflects a theme of change and transformation taking place in leaders as individuals, in their coworkers and in the organizations that bind them together in a common purpose. Transformational leaders take responsibility for revitalizing the corporation. They define the need for change, create new visions, mobilize commitment to those visions and ultimately transform the corporation.

THE VALUES THEORY BASIS FOR LEADERSHIP

Values are broad general beliefs about the way people should behave or some end state that they should attain. They are conclusive beliefs individuals develop about what is true or beautiful or good about the world. People form their values about the same way they develop personality. Values come out of early conditioning experiences and significant events. Most people's values are stabilized at an early age. By the time they reach adulthood, they have internalized a value system that serves them throughout their lives. Values, therefore, become statements of the "oughts" in our lives.

Two perspectives on the place of values in corporate life are applicable here. In one, the individual's values are preeminent, and organizations are formed to serve these values. The other idea suggests that organizations themselves have values that supersede those of individual members. Whether or not they emanate from the individual member or from the group, values shape group action, dictate reward systems and are the measures of individual and group success.

Several researchers have recognized the place of values in group life. Scott and Hart (1979) describe a generic corporate value system that they say prioritizes the value of corporate health. Values supporting this overarching value are those of rationality, efficiency, loyalty to the group and adaptability. Thayer (1980) sees values as operationally similar to objectives, goals, ends, purposes or policies. As corporation members accept a particular set of values and act upon them, they become the truth for them. Values that strengthen and perpetuate the corporation, and not the individual, may be the source of much of the pressure some see in corporate life.

For Burns (1978) values are standards that can be used to establish choices made, determine equity and balance policies and practices. In his seminal work on leadership, Burns also suggests that values can be a source of vital change in people and organizations. The central task is to manage values conflict in favor of a shared value system. Leaders appeal to widely held end values they and their followers come to esteem.

8

Principles of Values-based Leadership Theory

Values-based leadership theory is clear and uncomplicated. It is leader action to create a culture supportive of values that leads to mutual growth and enhanced self-determination. Implementation, however, requires a major shift in one's mind. Indeed, this is the centerpiece of values theory: adoption of a specific virtual environment that facilitates realization of these process and outcome desires. The true essence of leadership is not in procedures. It is in setting and teaching values to followers.

Of the many tasks all leaders have to do, some are more essential than others. There are structures to build and maintain, programs to manage, procedures to create and implement and policies to carry out. Furthermore, there are principles, values and expectations to honor and to teach to followers. Organizations, programs, procedures and policies can and do change. Principles are more enduring.

This model asks the leader to value coworkers in and of themselves, not just as parts of the production process. The principles of values-based leadership that follow from this new virtual environment are unique and give it practical vitality. They operationalize a people-oriented philosophy of growth toward self-leadership that involves learning and then teaching principles so followers can lead themselves.

Relating leadership behavior to programs, policies or other organizational factors is risky. As they change—and they always do—the requirements for leadership action change also. We risk being misled or misleading others as we overrely on these "physical" aspects of the corporation. Indeed, this is a fault of past leadership models. They constrain the leader into management systems, methods and processes and ignore the essential attitudes of mind and the value principles that are characteristic of leadership.

Relating his or her behavior to fundamental principles of life lets the leader survive even as details of the situation change. Leadership based on these principles allows the leader to lead group members over time. The fundamental values of leader-follower relationships are not responsive to fleeting situational vagaries. The leader's role becomes one of internalizing these value principles and teaching them to followers, who in turn, can internalize them in their independent actions. The result is to have independent followers capable of and desiring to, apply commonly held principles in their work. It is one of learning and then teaching principles so followers can lead themselves. As followers do this, they develop a loyalty toward the institution that cannot come in any other way.

CORE PRINCIPLES OF VALUES-BASED LEADERSHIP

Principle One: The Leader's Role is in Stakeholder Development

The novelty of this new leadership theory is in the philosophy of development that sustains it. It is a philosophy of (1) personal change toward high quality, (2) education of followers toward their potential for self-directed action and (3) creation of an environment conducive to self-directed, high-quality and innovative service.

This model sees the leader's role as transforming self, followers and the institution to achieve the vision in unique and creative ways. Once trained and committed, the leader shares responsibilities for action with followers. The goal of actions under this model is, in effect, to *let* followers lead themselves within the constraints of the shared vision. This kind of leadership is empowering. It seeks to expand the scope of personal control that followers enjoy by working collectively in the organization. It demonstrates authentic caring.

Leaders are enthusiastic supporters of their people. They love, encourage, enthuse and inspire employees and others to attain the organization's vision. They inculcate a strong service and quality work orientation in employees. They foster innovation, and they celebrate individual successes. They inspire coworkers by words, ideas and deeds that convey a sense of connection, excitement and shared commitment to group goals or methods.

Principle Two: The Leader's Role is to Create a Vision

The principal mechanism for implementing desired values and purposes is the vision statement. A vision statement is a short memorable motto or statement that encapsulates the core values the leader sets for the organization. In their behavior toward followers and others, leaders reflect these vision values. The values must be seen in leader actions such as goal setting, prioritizing activities, selecting and promoting staff and all other decisions and conduct.

The vision provides the basis for the leader's work to inspire stakeholders to self-directed action to realize it. The impact of this essential element is powerful. It pervades all else the leader does. It is the force binding leader and followers in a common purpose.

Principle Three: The Leader Creates a Culture Supportive of Core Values

Culture includes experiences, expectations for the future and values that condition behavior. Without general agreement on acceptable behavior and the value context within which they will operate, organization members are free to follow divergent paths. Coherent, cooperative action is impossible where agreement—at least implicitly—in a common culture is missing.

Creating and maintaining a culture conducive to attainment of personal and group goals is, therefore, a hallmark of leadership. Values-based leaders establish and maintain a culture that fosters this core-values vision and the other purposes of the leader. Creating a culture is a values-displacement activity. It is setting standards of conduct and performance that implement cultural values and behaviors. All of the leader's actions must be congruent with these values.

Principle Four: The Leader's Personal Preparation is in Individual One-on-One Relationships with Followers

Values-based leadership theory influences the leader's personal preparation and attitudes. True leadership is personal, intimate. It is many small acts involving the leader and individual followers. Leadership over large groups is possible. However, to be effective, individual group members must see it as a personal relationship. They must see a melding of their personal values with the leader's, their purposes with his, their methods with his.

Personal preparation in this model is essentially preparation to succeed in individual one-on-one relationships with followers. Leadership is, in essence, learning to sit in council with all stakeholders to insure understanding and acceptance of common values, work processes and goals. The sitting-in-council-with-followers relationship puts the leader and follower together in an equal, sharing relationship. Both—either— may propose the agenda, contribute ideas and methods to solve group problems or suggest new or altered program plans. Sitting in council with others is democratic and egalitarian.

Counseling, on the other hand, is unilateral action taken by the counselor toward the other person in the relationship. Counseling is telling; *counciling-with*[1] is finding out together what is right, proper and needed. Values leaders use followers as informal advisors to collaborate on policy, strategic decisions and overall program guidelines. The leader seeks opportunities and creates systems to share planning, decision making and work-methods determinations with individuals.

Principle Five: Values-based Leadership Asks the Leader to Be a Teacher

Leaders are primarily teachers of followers. Their role is to communicate with, inform and persuade followers to cooperative action. In all their behavior toward others, leaders teach the core-vision values they have set. Leader actions in goal setting, prioritizing work activity, selecting and promoting staff and all other decisions and actions should reflect and interpret the vision.

This leadership technology engages the leader in work to help followers change their relationships, work skills and attitudes. It is a task of straightforward teaching. It involves empowering followers, prioritizing high-quality service and fostering innovation. Leaders teach the vision, its values and goals and specific techniques to operationalize the vision, values and results. The leader's role is one of learning and then teaching principles and values so followers can lead themselves. As followers internalize principles of leadership, they develop a loyalty toward the corporation that cannot come in any other way.

Many see this teaching role as coaching. Coaching is one-on-one interaction with employees to teach, train and aid in the development of their skills, values and capacities. It is empowering of the individual. Coaching encourages independent action of employees. It focuses on the individual's strengths. While the principle of teaching emphasizes coaching, other techniques support this leadership principle.

---

[1]*Counciling-with* is a coined phrase meaning the leader's action of conferring with followers on equal terms.

Principle Six: The Values-based Leader Has the Dual Goal of Producing High-Performance and Self-led Followers

At least two results flow from leading based on shared values: enhanced skills and talents and more productive followers. The outcome desired is to have followers who are motivated by shared values and capable to act for themselves. Values-based leaders intend to create more leaders imbued with the same values and ideals who can work to realize vision goals and methods.

The values-based-leadership mental environment is unique in its emphasis on improving the individual follower's capacity for self-directed action to accomplish group goals. Both the context and technologies of this model move the follower toward this result as well as toward an improvement in performance. Success is attaining *both* results. Failing this, the leader must alter or improve either the context (culture) or the technology.

These principles constitute the philosophical base for values-based leadership. They define the essential elements of the philosophical basis for the values-based leadership mind-set. They are founded in common values that attract leaders and followers. They are not responsive to temporary changes in the situation. They work for the leader as well as the led. Both can find stability and consistency in the fundamental reasons for their association in the group, even in times of rapid change.

The leader's role is to teach core values to followers who use them in their work. Followers, in turn, can internalize these values in their independent actions. The result is to have independent followers capable of, and desiring to, apply commonly held values in all of their work relationships. As followers internalize principles of leadership, they develop a loyalty toward the corporation that cannot come in any other way.

9

The Values-based Leadership Model

The principles defined above describe the values-based-leadership virtual reality. They delineate its parameters and its scope. Leadership is fundamentally action. The values model shown in Figure 1 pictures how, and in what sequence, leadership action relying on these philosophical principles works. The principles served are highlighted in parentheses along with the major values served at each phase.

The five elements shown in Figure 1 represent the essence of this philosophy of leadership reality. The rest of this chapter elaborates on this model. Each element of the model relates directly to one or more of the six principles of this theoretical concept. The model relates the principles and connects them into an integrated whole. The values-based leadership movement of the past few years has developed out of these characteristics.

The view of leadership modeled below sees leadership as involved with several essential functions leading to (E) self-led, productive followers. These functions are (B) creation and maintenance of a cultural context supportive of excellent follower performance and (C) teaching and sitting in council with others to facilitate independent, high-quality, innovative follower performance. The leaders' virtual environment (A) is one of caring and development. The (D) vitalizing vision integrates culture and technologies and establishes the value needed to let members increase their capacities for self-direction.

Leadership has a special definition in values-based leadership. It includes designing, creating and working within a culture that fosters

Figure 1
The Values-based Leadership Model

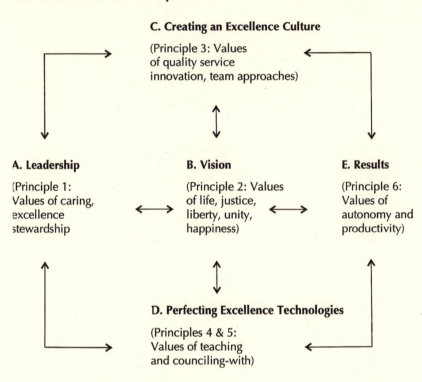

C. Creating an Excellence Culture

(Principle 3: Values
of quality service
innovation, team approaches)

A. Leadership

(Principle 1:
Values of caring,
excellence
stewardship

B. Vision

(Principle 2: Values
of life, justice,
liberty, unity,
happiness)

E. Results

(Principle 6:
Values of
autonomy and
productivity)

D. Perfecting Excellence Technologies

(Principles 4 & 5:
Values of teaching
and counciling-with)

the values and technologies implicit in a developmental virtual environment. The leaders' work is to develop themselves, their followers and their organizations. These ideas point to a new direction in defining and delimiting leadership. It centers on the critical task of helping in the development of all stakeholders.

ELEMENTS OF VALUES-BASED LEADERSHIP

The following elements define the nature of the values-based leadership virtual environment and are instructive in helping us think about this ideological foundation for leadership. They refine the model shown above.

Redefining Leadership

Success in implementing values-based leadership is based on a unique leadership reality that focuses on helping others become their best selves. Values-leaders prioritize the value of caring for others. They come to see the organization, its people and resources in stewardship terms—a jointly held, but temporary, service responsibility. As stewards, leaders take as a prime responsibility the need to care for and improve both the people they work with and the team they collectively represent.

Creating the Values-based Leadership Culture

Creating and maintaining a culture conducive to accomplishment of personal and group goals is a hallmark of values-based leadership. It is a values-displacement activity. Culture includes experience, expectations for the future and values that condition behavior. The values explicit in the culture define the working context of values-based leadership.

Values-based leadership depends on the ambient culture for legitimacy and as the vehicle for communicating and enforcing desired values. Without general agreement on acceptable behavior and the value context within which they will operate, team members are free to follow divergent paths. Coherent, cooperative action is impossible where common agreement—at least implicitly—is missing. Leaders create this culture, which is supportive of desired values.

Visioning

Leaders create a vision of present and future potential for the team and its people and then enrolls them in that vision. The vision provides the basis for the leader's action to inspire stakeholders to self-directed action to realize that vision. This task affects all else the leader does.

Visioning emphasizes the central values and possibilities that define the group and constitute its niche in society. The vision activates deeply held beliefs about what the individual and the society is all about. It is an invisible force binding leader and followers in a common purpose. Visions reflect deeply held beliefs accepted by most people in the culture. They hark back to the core values that established American society and the ideals about what organized group action should entail. Values-based leadership in America is based on a few powerful values that are effectively summarized in the Preamble to the U.S. Constitution, the Declaration of Independence and similar core documents.

In many respects these founding values define deeply held beliefs about what group action should be like. They strike a responsive chord in most people. Organizations that do not foster them are seen as somehow wrong, improper, faulty. They provided the original rationale for the founding of the United States and the construction of its basic institutions. They also provide the values-context within which the group's work is done.

The five founding values below represent some of the essential values critical in vision setting in America. While one may be spotlighted, all five should be respected, at least implicitly, in the culture supporting any vision.

Respect for Life

Protection of life, concern for the quality of life and respect for each person's right to safety, security and protection are important, valuable and honorable. Leaders that translate these founding values in their vision in ways that respect the humanity of people and trust in their essential goodness find that this energizes followers. Reflecting this value in vision statements let followers commit more fully to the work and the group than can less fundamental values.

Liberty or Freedom of Choice

Americans value the opportunity for independent action. Freedom consists of several capacities. One is the innate capacity to choose. Freedom is also the power to will to do as we ought. It also consists of circumstantial freedom, or freedom constrained by the details of the situation, which vary over time. Leaders that incorporate this founding value into their vision statement and protect it in their culture enlist the cooperation and commitment of followers. In this way, they can incorporate the power of the larger community culture into their group's means-and-ends strategy.

Justice

Justice, equality and fairness: these ideas are explicit in American society and its institutions and operations. Sometimes leaders have honored some of these ideas more in the breach than in fact. Nonetheless, they represent deeply held beliefs about how leaders should treat people. Justice translated into the team connotes ideas of fairness to all group members. Programs that include respect for the individual rights of group members and fairness in application of rules, whether applied to members or clients, gain adherents.

Unity

Sharing in a common enterprise characterized by some of these founding values excites and commits people. Adler (1969) confirms that to love and be loved and to be respected by others with whom we associate are basic innate human needs. Leaders need to recognize this innate human need for affiliation, either implicitly or explicitly, in their strategic group visions.

Happiness

Happiness is the aim of life. It is the ultimate good in philosophy. All other needs contribute to our happiness (Adler, 1969). Happiness connotes a situation of respect for, and encouragement of, these needs. Organizations whose cultures recognize the innate need people have to seek and find happiness attract people. Most people expect our organizations to honor this basic need and value and to incorporate this value into corporate life. Those that do not recognize, at least minimally, this innate desire find that their workers expend energy in seeking happiness at the expense of the group.

RESULTS OF THE VALUES-BASED LEADERSHIP PHILOSOPHY

The former, less complete, virtual-leadership environments sought improved follower performance measured in corporate goal terms. They each argued that their brand of leadership would result in enhanced productivity. In each of these models the worker remains a labor slave of the corporation and leader; workers are essentially cast as tools to help achieve the leader's corporate or personal goals.

Since values-based leadership is a relatively new model guiding leader action, little empirical research has been done to quantify the results emanating from leadership according to these principles. One recent interesting and informative study shows that productivity improvements result when leaders are present in line organizations (Jernigan, 1997). Michael Jernigan studied approximately 200 first-line laborers, their supervisors and top departmental executives in a medium-size public works organization in a southern city. According to his findings, leader-led work crews produced more work per unit of output than their manager-led counterparts.

Using standard survey instruments, personal observation and self-developed questionnaires, Jernigan identified work crew supervisors as either managers or leaders based on worker and supervisor perceptions of their bosses' success in developing trust and insuring values congruence. He then measured productivity of all work crews over a three-year time span. Invariably leader-led crews outperformed their manager-led counterparts. The improvement ranged from 3 percent to 479 percent. This study is a powerful argument that leadership based on commonly shared values can and does make both human and financial sense.

Acceptable bottom-line performance is a given in any corporate relationship. The values-based leader, however, has the dual goal of producing high performance *and* highly developed, self-led followers. This leadership principle accepts productivity as a goal. However, it also focuses on the equally vital goal of helping followers attain their personal self-development aims for independent action. As far as the organization's work allows, the leader maximizes follower talents for the sake of *both* the bottom line and the individual.

SUMMARY

Values-based leadership is unique in its emphasis on improving the individual follower's capacity to lead himself or herself. Both the context and technology of this model move the follower toward this result along with performance improvement. The culture fostered by the leader aids in realization of this principle. The vision must include this outcome. So, too, must the techniques and skills employed. Success is defined by attaining both outcomes. Failing this, either the context (culture) or the technology (methods) must be improved.

PART IV

Trust Leadership

The leader-follower relationship is essentially voluntary. Followers need not respond to leadership in the same way that employees obey their manager's orders. Leaders often cannot use force or coercion to attain their ends, nor do they want to. To gain the use of their followers' talent, time and imagination means leaders must influence them to *want* to do what needs to be done. No one can force creativity or commitment. Leadership is a process of building a trust culture within which leader and follower can relate in accomplishing mutually valued goals using agreed-upon processes.

Much of current group culture works against needed internal unity and cohesion. Multiple competing cultures with their different value systems are the norm today. They are challenging traditional workplace cultures both from within and without. It stretches our collective imagination to suggest that a leader can, by dint of personality or capacity, unite a group of diverse individuals and groups long enough to produce anything consistently. The task is simply beyond the capacity of any one leader. This is especially true when effort is also directed to respect, honor and preserve largely intact each cultural sub-set's unique values, customs and traditions.

10

Unified Cultures

Part of the present leadership problem is that we have thought of leadership in terms of the individual leader. We have accepted a charismatic leader model exemplified by an individual with special traits or skills. We have charged this super-leader with the task of shaping our social organizations.

Our model for social change also is faulty. The conventional wisdom is that, to change individuals, leaders need only change the formal structure or work systems. We think that new programs, new people, new equipment, computerization or detailed procedures, strong rules or laws will produce needed change.

Externally imposed change is effective, but only if we use coercive control over coworkers. This change model denigrates individual workers and treats them as interchangeable parts, "cogs" in the corporate machine. Workers are asked to change as the organization's leader sees a need, whether or not they want to, are ready, or even capable of the proposed change.

A more successful method is to change individuals first and then let them change the formal structure. Unfortunately, not all leaders have adopted this model because, while it is more sure and long-lasting, it is also slower and less predictable in the short run. And it asks leaders to give up personal control and devolve it to the individual and the team.

Fortunately, leaders are coming to see their role in change as a task of creation, not control. Values-based leaders are creating trust cultures to undergird both personal and institutional growth. The trust culture provides a unifying context within which leaders and followers work and focus effort toward agreed-upon goals, values and vision ideals. The effect is to inspire the formal structure to change.

Seeing leadership as a sharing, not a starring, role is different from past leadership virtual environments. Shaping a culture in which group members can trust each other enough to work together lets leaders create the mental and physical context within which they can lead, followers can find reason for full commitment and both can achieve their potential.

A harmonious culture is the basis of leadership. Of all the new and pressing problems leaders face daily one stands out. It is the challenge of creating and maintaining a corporate culture that fits the nature of the work done *and* the character and capacities of the increasingly diverse work force. It is a problem of the integration of the worker and the organization so the system meets the needs of both.

Leadership is not so much a function of the individual as it is a condition of the culture. While spontaneous at times, lasting leadership is a result of specific planned actions to create a culture characterized by internal harmony and based on values and ideals the leader and follower have come to share. Leadership is the task of creating harmony among the disparate, sometimes competing, organizational, human and program factions. It is an expression of community.

Notwithstanding this, many theorists value personal independence and difference over collective interdependence. The effect is to thwart leadership. Leaders flourish in situations where they and their followers share unifying values, ideals and goals. They are successful only when they unite individuals in collaborative action without losing too much of the individual freedom they and their followers want.

Active, dynamic leadership is scarce in American society and its institutions. We find depressingly few people who others acknowledge as leaders in either government, business, social or religious realms. Those that do come to mind are all too often older and represent former times and ideals. It is not individual leaders that are lacking. Rather, the culture that makes leadership possible is missing from society. Few current local, regional, national or global organizations can boast of these qualities and characteristics. Hence the dearth of leaders.

Collaborative action and individual freedom are qualities that describe the leadership environment, a unified, harmonious culture characterized by mutual trust that allows leadership to take place. The key to leadership is a corporate context where leader and led share values and vision. Leadership can only take place within a context where both leaders and followers can be free to trust the purposes, actions and intent of others. The real purpose of corporate culture is to create a climate of mutual trust within which all persons can grow and develop to their full potential as leaders and followers. It is only in a culture of shared trust that leadership can evolve and flourish.

There is little hope that blind acceptance of multiple and diverse internally competing value systems will produce stable, effective and responsive, economic, social or governmental organizations. The likelihood is that all that will be produced is balkanization. There is even less hope that a situation of unrestrained cultural diversity will result in a cure for our social ills and restore a nurturing culture that most Americans can accept.

The leadership challenge of the new millennium is in the realms of the mind. Leadership has always been mental. Tomorrow it will be even more a matter of changing the way people think and the measures they use to evaluate personal and group performance. Leadership based on trust is a mind-changing activity involving leaders in transforming peoples' way of viewing their work relationship. It is a culture-building task, but a special kind of culture-building based on mutual interactive trust.

THE IMPACT OF CULTURE ON LEADERSHIP

Culture is a powerful force. It directs our lives and our relationships with group members. Strong cultures act as intellectual and emotional paradigms (Barker, 1992) that can block acceptance of alternative cultures. Cultural paradigms can isolate the individual member from other cultural groups—coworkers, family, church and the larger community. On the other hand, they can also unite individuals into strong coalitions of mutually interdependent teams.

Finding a common value basis for cooperative interaction is the preeminent challenge of leaders today. However, the task is not so daunting as it may appear. Most people share certain principles, values and beliefs in common. These principles and values transcend subculture, race, religion or nationality. They represent something more than mere preference or belief. They provide a common bond upon which we base our trust of another person.

Common values build trust, and trust is the foundation of cooperative action. The kind of leadership that grows out of shared values only flourishes in a climate within which individuals can accept the individuality of others without sanctioning all of their behavior or words. In a climate of trust, individuals can give open, candid reactions to what they see as right or wrong. In trust cultures there is little manipulation, few hidden agendas, no unreasonable controls, no saccharine sweetness that discounts real problems. Instead, there is a congruency in concepts, conduct and concern: a unity appropriate to group membership that does not risk individuality. Without trust, cultural values can become strictures, impeding individual and group progress.

It does very little good, for instance, to develop elaborate corporate work flow charts if the people who inhabit the real world symbolized by these charts do not trust one another or really communicate. It does little good to strive to achieve goals if leaders allow themselves to be too much at the mercy of their moods so followers see them as ambivalent administrators who are unpredictable or capricious about the goals mutually embraced.

THE IMPACT OF TRUST ON CULTURE AND ON LEADERSHIP

From a corporate perspective, the problem of culture creation and maintenance is one of leadership. Creating the kind of physical and psychological environment necessary to get others to *want* to follow them taxes leaders' ability on all levels. The task of creating a corporate culture that engages both the emotions and the best efforts of members and coordinates them into a unity is hard. At its core, it is a problem of developing trust.

Once given, trust opens opportunities for us to gain experiences with another person or thing. That is, we increase trust by the acquisition of more true knowledge about, let us say, a person. We diminish it by the same process: acquisition of information that belies our initial perception of the truth about the person that formed the basis of our initial trust actions.

The process of gaining trust relies first on having or securing some accurate knowledge of the person, thing or situation. Gaining this intimate knowledge forms the basis of a lasting trust. It is encouraged by a culture that values trust *per se*, that honors the individual and that fosters cooperative interaction. Leadership is a task of building unifying, values-based trust cultures more than it is charisma, communication or crisis management.

Unless the culture reflects and is supportive of common values, leadership based on such values is impossible. Culture determines a large part of what leaders do and how they do it. Culture also determines corporate practice and confirms that practice. In actuality leadership is a consequence of corporate culture, and culture is a result of leadership (Wildavsky, 1984). The two are intertwined.

INTEGRATING VALUES IN CULTURE

We can define individual success in organizations in terms of fit with the prevailing culture. We realize a fit when individual behavior conforms to prevailing cultural values, when it becomes conventional. Ultimately, all culture is convention. It is putting design and shape into the common environment, beginning in the mind. A culture is a self-contained virtual environment that we see as conventional. Conventions are rule-bound, internally complete and values-laden. Conventions separate, distinguish and isolate this culture from other cultures, teaching us to value some things as opposed to others.

Corporate or individual values are part of a system, or set, of variously rated values that guide our life and actions and that make that action predictable. Most people's values are similar to those of the people around them, in their common cultural surround. Values constitute a network of known and shared understandings and norms that we take for granted. They provide a base of commonality in community life.

Values are the settled beliefs that guide our actions and judgements of what is good, right and appropriate. Group values represent those truths all or most members of a community share and know they should seek after (whether they do or not). We accept group values because they are good for us and because we feel that they will result in greater material, moral or spiritual development. Commonly shared values are the foundation of trust between individuals. Shared values also form the basis for mutual trust between groups, whether nations, communities or corporate cultures.

Values are an important part of human experience. They can be personal, professional, corporate or societal. Values define both what ought to be and what is in our lives (Schein, 1985; Sathe, 1983). Cultural beliefs inside our organizations cover a wide range of topics (Lorsch, 1986). At the core is the values system of top leaders. These values often find voice in a vision statement around which the corporation and its leaders interact. Vision values set the direction and limits of the group's capabilities.

Corporate values, and the culture that gives them context, direct and open some possibilities and inhibit others. They need to be set, maintained, changed as needed and constantly kept relevant to present action and plans. Culture is both an individual and a collective human phenomenon. Leaders need to understand and use the corporate cultural values to insure member commitment. A common set of values binds people together. Conflicting values affect work behavior and attitudes. They disrupt and may even destroy a corporation or other work team.

Values are powerful parts of our virtual environment that prescribe rules and regulate worker actions. We do not develop a trust culture as a byproduct of routinely developed and changed programs. Trust is neither a new program nor a result of a series of "new programs." People will not continue to offer their commitment to leaders who continually present new programs—which are really rehashes of the same basic paradigm—to accomplish the same task. Rather programs that implicitly or explicitly prioritize values and are conducted consistently in terms of those values best illustrate a trust culture.

11

Defining Culture

We can make several assumptions about culture. First, it exists. Every organization and group that endures for even a modestly short time develops a culture, and each culture is largely unique. Second, it provides members with a method of understanding events, symbols and messages formed within the group and unique to it. Third, culture is a kind of lever for directing group behavior; it is a control mechanism approving or prohibiting some behaviors and shaping others.

Organizations are about how much members trust each other, if indeed they trust others at all. They are about attitudes and emotions and their impact on team performance. Organizations are definable best in these terms and in ideas like change, trust, cohesion, conformity and adaptability. In a word, they are about culture.

All organizations are definable in terms of culture. Organizational culture is distinct from corporate strategy, structure and work processes. Of course, there is value in looking at corporations from the perspective of physical facilities, structure, systems of workflow and the tools and equipment used. But, the corporation is mostly about people in interaction. Corporations are about the collective values people hold about the common enterprise.

The leader's task is to create a culture that integrates all individuals into a natural unity so individual actions can strengthen the results of the whole. When the prevailing culture is incompatible with the leader's vision, the task is to change the culture to insure that it promotes needed integration and harmony. Leadership is changing people and artifacts to find unity in apparent chaos (Wheatley, 1993). This idea is especially important as leaders begin to lead in cultures peopled by widely diverse individuals. Making these culturally diverse people a part of a harmonious whole has always been the prime task of leaders.

Culture has a long history as a means of identifying and rating social groups. It has a short history as a means for defining and comparing corporate work teams. We can think of culture in hierarchical or systems terms. That is, a given corporate culture may contain several subcultures. Each can differ in some respects from each other and from the parent. Knowing the parameters of the larger culture helps in defining and analyzing the details of the subcultures making up the larger body.

Successful cultures are characterized by enough mutual trust and respect to let members be free to make choices, to empower them to meet at least some of their needs. Command and control systems and structures typical of past industrial-age business and government bureaucracies seldom provide that trust or that freedom, except perhaps at the very top levels. This argues against traditional tight managerial control. What we need today are trained, focused and committed workers whom leaders can trust to respond appropriately in rapidly changing situations where top-level oversight is not desirable or, sometimes, even possible. Such a new culture is one that focuses more on results than on process. Leadership in this changing social and cultural environment must change too.

The dimension of this cultural change is as broad and comprehensive as the corporation itself. Some critical dimensions of corporate life with practical cultural implications include the following:

Communications. Organizations operate on information exchanges between people and work units. Communication is the nerve system of the organization. It is a complex system that can be blocked at many levels and in many forms.

Cooperation. Chester Barnard (1968) identified attaining cooperation as a critical executive function. Fostering cooperation is one of the prime challenges leaders face in modern sociotechnical systems.

Control. Control over work and workers is a prime outcome of the formal structure. It is an interpersonal process that involves rules, procedures and sanctions. It involves our individual needs and wishes for power to exert influence over others as well as feelings about others' control over us.

Conflict. Conflict is a part of day-to-day life in organizations. It is seen in intrapersonal and interpersonal interactions. Conflict is ignored in many traditional organizations or dealt with through rules. Seen as a factor in control, culture ties in with ideas of esteem, reward systems and a host of motivations and values.

Commitment. Achieving the commitment of followers is a hallmark of leadership. Some elements of this task include clear, known goals, personal belief in these goals and pride in their achievement.

Cohesiveness. Similar to commitment, cohesiveness connotes strong identification with the group or task, feelings of support from the relationship and a desire to stay with the team and keep it together. Cohesiveness comes as people share common values, common skills or a common vision. Structure, system and procedure alone do not build a sense of cohesiveness and unity. That comes as members invest in, and take ownership of, the corporation and its aims and purposes.

Trust. The level of trust present in the group determines the extent people can be themselves—say what is on their mind, try out tentative ideas, express anger or joy. Organizations with low trust levels create "yes people," conformists who contribute little to moving the team forward.

Caring. People differ in their need for close personal relations with others. Some are cool and distant; others are warm and intimate. The culture of the team, rather than the formal structure or the operating system, helps define the acceptable level of concerned intimacy in the organization.

These operating processes interact to form the social aspects of the organization. Other factors are also present in any corporate culture and may change behavior and ultimate success. Indeed, any aspect of the corporate relationship or any external factors impinging on team performance can modify corporate culture. Thus, professionalism, personal or professional biases and social or corporate politics can be features of culture. Similarly, task or system complexity, changing work values, training and development, task design and task assignment systems are also cultural determinants. Each of these factors is also present in most organizations. These cultural factors can influence how people respond to the requirements of the work system.

ELEMENTS OF DEFINITION

Most people's definition of organizational or corporate culture includes elements like shared values, beliefs, assumptions, patterns of relationships and behaviors. Uttal (1983) explicitly defines culture as a system of shared values and beliefs that interacts with team members, corporate structures and control systems to produce behavioral norms that aid feelings of cooperation, trust and security.

Corporate culture can be thought of as a pattern of basic assumptions that has developed over time as a result of coping with external and internal problems in the environment (Schein, 1985). Seen in this way, the organization's culture is founded in core values and beliefs that have evolved in a team over time (Nadler and Tushman, 1988). These core values are imbedded in generally known and understood statements about what is good or not good about an organization.

Corporate core values define acceptable behavior as well as acceptable traits or characteristics. The core values become "if-then" belief systems. "If we behave in this way, then something good will result," or "If we value this idea, then we can expect acceptance from the group." They constrain and direct member behavior in predictable ways.

We can define culture simply as the commitment and order in a social team that allows people to trust one another enough to work together. These characteristics are also fostered through the whole of the culture's beliefs, ideology, language, ritual and myth systems. Leaders and followers create the assumptions, symbols, languages, beliefs, visions, ideologies and myths of the organization. These features of culture let members understand one another, trust one another and take personal ownership of the group's activities.

We can look at culture from two mental viewpoints. First, culture is the overarching system of settled beliefs that defines the person or institution initially and gives direction to daily life. Culture prescribes the general ways people relate to one another—whether in trusting or distrusting ways. This is a strategic, global perspective and proceeds from both internal and external guiding beliefs. Second, culture is about the daily routine of a given organization. Culture defines the accepted system of meanings (derived from guiding beliefs) that give direction to specific routine daily acts.

Corporate culture refers to the deep-set beliefs about the way that we should structure any organization or team (corporate, community or national) and the way we should exercise authority, reward, control and interrelate with people. Culture consists of a set of cognitive reference points that form a framework within which team members can interpret the meaning of their own behavior.

Corporate culture also consists of the basic common assumptions of team or group members. It includes the history of corporate experience, whom members trust and to what degree and how the team solves problems. And, it is about what the team considers a problem in the first place. Culture defines how a particular group has adapted to its environment. Culture is real, if often assumed and implicit rather than explicit. It defines the nature and character of the organization.

Corporate culture includes both historical precedent and present experience. It defines both current and future expectations. It organizes the values that condition behavior. Without general agreement on acceptable behavior and the value context within which we will operate, team members are free to follow divergent paths. Indeed, no coherent, cooperative action is possible where common agreement—at least implicitly—in a core culture is missing.

Leadership is a function of the habits of interrelationship developed in a group. It develops out of the dynamics of the interaction between followers and between a follower and the tasks assigned. Leaders facilitate joint activity by accommodating difference, by *redirecting* it to joint action. Leadership is only possible in situations where people trust each other enough to be open and honest about their needs and the tension between those needs and organizational needs.

The leader-created culture in turn determines the leader's reality. It prescribes what leaders pay attention to, their reaction to member behavior, what is communicated (taught) to followers; it is the living model of the corporation they project to others. The leader both creates and is constrained by, the culture created and its values. The culture sets the pattern for mutual interrelationships.

Leadership is a values-displacement activity (Fairholm, 1991). It is a task of creating teams unified by a common mind-set about purpose and values that both leader and led can use to measure group and personal progress. The leader-created culture embodies institutional purpose (Selznick, 1957). Leaders preach it to others and behave personally according to it. They attain follower support because the attitudes and purposes they articulate come to mean as much to group members as they do to the leader.

12

Shaping Culture

Organizations develop cultures that incorporate the values, practices and ways of thinking of their leaders. Culture evolves through the accumulation of actions and events the members of a team experience. Leaders play an essential role in this maturation process. They, more than any other participant, are critical in structuring experiences for team members that point them toward desired results.

Leaders emphasize some experiences over others and in this way further focus the cultural integration process. It is a process of changing the way people thing about their work, their coworkers and their joint purposes. Creating a corporate culture involves leaders in several important mind-changing tasks. Among them are setting the values base for mutual interaction and thinking strategically about the team and its future. It is systematically shaping a desired culture within which members can trust others and expect others to trust them.

TECHNIQUES FOR SHAPING CULTURE

Shaping Culture through Shaping Values

Leadership is a culture-building, value-infusing, mind-changing activity (Selznick, 1957). The values group members share act to support member interactions respecting accepted levels of trust, the right level of commitment and the strength of that commitment. Establishing shared values is the first and most crucial culture-setting leadership task.

The values thus set become the basis for a corporate virtual environment that guides subsequent individual and group interaction. While leaders shape values, they are made manifest in the culture through attitudes fostered and rites, rituals, myths, strategies and goals assumed. Values establish the foundation for more specific operational and interpersonal work standards used by the group.

Shaping Culture through Strategic Planning

Strategies are the source of cohesiveness in the team (Eadie, 1983). Strategic planning is a way to concentrate group resources on what leaders see as horizon issues. Strategic planning is actually a focusing and a reduction of interest, not a broadening and generalizing of interest. Strategic plans operationalize a self-definition of what the corporation and its people want to be in the future. The purpose of strategic planning is to integrate action of different corporate units and enable headquarters units to capitalize on the resulting synergies. It lets individuals and subgroups better understand their various roles and relationships.

Shaping Culture through Communication

Culture helps us create a situational context where empathy between the partners in the communication exchange is possible. Communicating this empathy is dependent on both the sender and the receiver sharing certain essential cultural parameters, such as language, experiences and values. Communicating intended meaning is only done between people who share a common mind-set about essential values and behaviors.

Shaping Culture through Office Politics

Office politics, like regular politics, is the art of who gets what, when and how (Lasswell and Kaplin, 1950). While some denigrate the practice of office politics, it is nevertheless an integral part of corporate life (Fairholm, 1993). It is conditioned by and reflects the ambient culture. It is the basis for much of the interpersonal activity we engage in on the job. The character of the culture conditions our use of office politics. The culture determines the precise nature of the adjustments we make in our relationships with others to get our way.

Shaping Desired Organizational Action

Culture guides member's actions and expectations about how to act and think, who to trust and what to hate or honor. Culture interprets the actions of members, defines the level of trust and respect members ought to have for one another and sanctions behavior that violates cultural norms. It lets members know what to value and how to feel about certain actions or events. Culture defines and maintains corporate borders. It affects individual and team performance directly and indirectly (Ott, 1989).

Shaping Effectiveness Levels

Schein (1985) says culture constrains corporate strategy. Odom, Boxx and Dunn (1990) suggest that it affects employee satisfaction and commitment, work team cohesion, strategy implementation and corporate performance. The culture determines, in large part, the level of effectiveness the group determines is needed. It also defines the level of commitment, satisfaction and cohesion of the team members (Steers, 1985). These factors are essential aids to the flexibility and adaptability essential in today's world.

Shaping Attitudes

Culture provides and defines the emotional ambience, the attitudes within which team members work. The local culture helps or inhibits a shared mind-set that circumscribes how people feel about what they do, why they do it and the level of excellence they will seek. Cultural attitudes permeate the workplace and constrain individual and team feelings about what is and is not okay.

Shaping Change

Culture leadership teaches that the fastest, most effective and most long-lasting way to get institutional change is to deal with people face-to-face and get them to accept altered cultural values and work expectations. Cultures change as people change their values, beliefs, assumptions, expectations and their resultant actions. It is not laws, rules, or management, that change society. It is the result of many individual actions that changes us. As we choose to accept a new way to think and value life, we adopt new behaviors and new attitudes and these things change us.

The only real change occurs when individuals independently change themselves. The group's formal structures and institutions change after this personal change. The challenge of leadership is to foster and direct this personal change. Of course changing the circumstances can eventually change people's minds and hearts. But this is a secondary technology. It ignores values and attitudes in favor of the artifacts, rather than the heart, of culture.

Culture provides meaning, direction and social energy that moves the firm into either productive action, mediocrity or destruction. Sometimes the culture becomes a counterpoint to the formal top management policy and structure. When it does, we waste available energy as workers devote time to both sets of values, ideologies and socio-emotional activities. The impact of a group culture on its members is powerful, and when it is opposed to the formally articulated corporate strategy, it can become a stumbling block.

13

The Leadership of Trust

Trust is central to leadership in organizations because followers are people who *choose* to follow leaders. They are not forced to do so. Being trusted by followers allows leaders to lead. Low-trust cultures reduce the willingness of members to volunteer to follow. Therefore, these low-trust cultures need to use control mechanisms to secure member compliance. That is, *low-trust cultures force us to manage, not lead.*

The idea of trust has been given very little specific attention by either theoretical or practicing professionals. The culture created by leaders produces a trust situation where we can trust certain actions to produce certain results. It also prescribes our willingness to trust. One culture may allow us to trust others more or less than another, but without the restraints imposed by cultural features we could not exercise trust at all.

Leaders build trust or tear it down by the cumulative actions they take and the words they speak—by the culture they create for themselves and their organization's members. The cumulative effect of a given culture is to define a specific level and quality of interpersonal trust between members.

Organizational theory assumes, but largely ignores, the idea of trust. Nevertheless, it is integral to that set of interpersonal relationships that produces trust. Trust places an obligation on both the truster and the person in whom trust is placed. It is the foundation of success in leadership or any interpersonal relationship. Trust implies proactivity. With trust we can act in an otherwise unknown, ambiguous, even risky, situation. Without trust the individual has no power in relationships, no control over other people not actually in sight. Trust is central to empowerment, expectation and predictability. Without at least some assurance that information, actions or events are real, trust is extremely risky.

We build our lives on trust relationships. Our actions apply trust or its lack in everything we do or say. We trust others to obey basic traffic rules. We trust stores to honor our credit cards. We trust maintenance people to repair our appliances. All aspects of the working relationship, our corporate work cultures, are based on trust of others—superiors, peers, subordinates, customers and other stakeholders.

Trust or its lack is at the heart of many of the problems society presents to the thoughtful observer. Much of social culture today is fragmented and conflict-ridden. Leadership in this kind of environment requires adherence to ethical principles that highlight trust (Maccoby, 1981). This kind of principle-based society is missing today. Sadly, people appear to have lost confidence in their leaders and in the programs that they lead.

We have lost the sense of community that former cultures provided. Now people are together, but as individuals, not as a community. Many of our business organizations and even some of our families lack the cohesion that mutual trust provides. One result is that many people suffer from isolation, anomie and anxiety. Unless workers trust not only the leaders' motives, but also their ability to lead, they will not follow (Hitt, 1988).

In the past, reliance on structural form or workflow processes has done something to improve efficiency. This focus alone largely ignores the socio-psychological dimensions of corporate life. Yet, it is in this socio-psychological dimension of team interrelationships that we can find the solution to many contemporary problems. It is trust more than either power or hierarchy that makes a team function effectively (Barnes, 1981).

Leaders need to be aware of both the existence and the potential significance of trust in established cultural beliefs and norm systems. They should learn to identify and alter those cultural norms that act to limit trust. Once shaped, cultural values and norms provide the base against which we can measure changes in organizational activities and assess potential changes to determine the level of interactive trust present. Trust can help us lessen conflicts and avoid potential conflicts before dysfunctional behavior takes place.

THE TRUST-TRUTH MODEL

Trust is, in essence, based on the truth. The information on which we base our trusting behaviors must eventually prove accurate if we are to expect success now and in the future. The people we trust to do their jobs professionally must, in fact, perform competently, or we withdraw our trust. The future we rely on must come to pass, or our plans (and the planning process) are meaningless. Unless the past is prologue to today—and tomorrow—we do not trust today's actions and events. Our leap of faith to trust another must pay off in reality, or we lose interest and sever our association.

Trust and an eventually proved reality are inseparable. Properly placed trust empowers us. Misplaced trust spells defeat. Trust is effective only if we use it in terms of an ultimate reality—a reality that eventually will prove true in practice. We exercise in terms of the truth—the reality—trusted in. To trust one must have some evidence, some clue, an assumption, at least, about what the truth is.

Trust is a social expectation. It is a condition of the situation as much as it is of a human relationship. The expectations and assumptions members hold about how much risk they can (or should) accept in working with others in situations where full knowledge is not present shape our relationships.

To trust another person or thing means that we have confidence that we will eventually confirm that what we see (or hope for) in that person or thing is the truth about them. It is a hope based on factors in a person, or the situational context. Thus, trust is, or can be, a logical, thoughtful expectation. It need not be blind.

Trust, as a word and as an idea, connotes feelings of security, confidence, self-reliance, intimacy and integrity in the absence of hard proof. To be trustworthy is to be dependable, deserving of confidence, reliable, faithful, believable—one whom others see as a person with a firm belief in honesty and justice.

Barber (1983) says trust has to do with the expectations people have about something. It follows our acceptance of an assumed truth about another person or thing. Our trust continues and is sustained and enlarged only as future experiences confirm that early perception to be, in fact, correct. That is, trust builds as experience proves the essential truth of our initial perceptions. Trust diminishes by the reverse. As people or things are proved less than, or different from, our initial perceptions, we withdraw out trust.

In essence, trust can only be given; it cannot be commanded. Trusting people are willing volunteers. Trust is an interactive, interdependent process of taking a risk to trust, gaining experience and then enlarging or diminishing trust as that experience proves our initial perception to be true or false. The key to a trust relationship is the continued willingness of someone to follow based on his or her experience. It is a noncompulsory relationship.

According to this definition of trust, we are all continually engaged in trusting relationships. Farmers plant seed without a total assurance that a harvest will result. We marry without knowing the full truth about our partner. We delegate work to subordinates or accept our leader's instructions without knowing their full importance or relevance to our personal concerns or responsibilities. We exercise faith in a Supreme Being without visual or tactile contact. Yet we engage in these relationships and countless others daily, trusting that most of the time we will not misplace our trust: that is, trusting that the person or thing trusted will prove to be true.

DEVELOPING TRUST

Developing trust is difficult. Haney (1973) says to trust is to take a chance on the other person. It is a risk relationship; it increases our vulnerability (Zand, 1972). Trust and distrust are cyclical. The more one trusts, the more trusting the relationship. And, alternatively, the more one distrusts others, the more distrust is present.

People cannot demand trust of another. It must be earned, and that takes time. While leaders can ask others for their trust, they cannot enforce that demand simply because they have the authority to hire and fire. Trust is a gift, given freely by others because it is based on their confidence in us, their respect, even their admiration for us.

Trust is a range of observable behaviors and feelings that encompasses predictability (Rossiter and Pearch, 1975). Trust behavior shows a willingness to be vulnerable to another. Trust is reflected in an attitude of faith or confidence in the other person. This faith is such that we believe the other person will behave in ways that will not produce negative results for us.

Trust implies more than confidence (Gibb, 1978). It is an unquestioned belief. Confidence implies trust based on good reasons, evidence or experience. Open non-defensive interpersonal communications with others build trust.

Self-trust produces trustworthiness. It helps insure loyalty, cooperation, efficiency and satisfaction. Our willingness to change is dependent largely on the trust levels present in our relationships with others in the group (or groups) in which we find ourselves. Feelings of trust develop initially by the way in which two people interact. These feelings become established only after a series of incidents that prove the intrinsic level of trust in the relationship.

Self-trust comes because of several characteristics we exhibit. Among them the following are the most important: knowledge, responsibility and faith. Knowledge refers to the stored truth we gain from learning and experience. Responsibility defines individuals' acceptance of accountability for themselves and for their work and other actions. Faith is confidence in the correctness, the appropriateness, of our course of action and our abilities to attain desired goals.

Several factors are critical in understanding how we develop trust, nurture it and expand it. Among them are integrity, patience, altruism, vulnerability, action, friendship, character, competence and judgement (Fairholm, 1994b). We trust people who demonstrate these qualities more, and more often, than others who do not reflect these qualities. These factors define the individual. They are also characteristics of corporate culture that make it suitable for mutual trusting interactions.

Trust begets trust. We have to trust to become trusted. People base their trust of others on expectations developed from past contacts with individuals or with groups or things generally (Good, 1988). Sometimes we give our trust to another in novel situations. This is fragile and may not necessarily be a mutual trust. A more durable, full and mutual trust is contingent upon full communications, need-satisfaction and experience with others that includes their living up to our expectations over time.

When leaders understand and appreciate a follower's efforts, they are bestowing trust on that follower (Culbert and McDonough, 1985). This kind of respect for individual differences is the key to the trust relationship, for trust comes from, and is developed out of, the context of shared respect for differences, rather than from dependency. At least four approaches to developing trust are available. Each has something to offer to our overall understanding of trust, its development and maturation and the ways people apply and use it in our formal and informal relationships. These four approaches include ideas of participation, helping, listening and leadership.

Developing Trust through Participation

Trust is encouraged and fostered by shared experiences. The sharing can be a sharing of experiences, or it can be a sharing of ideas or philosophies. Leaders acting out of an authentic participative leadership style provide a culture that encourages trust in them and in the joint enterprise. A participative leadership style also includes shared decision making, encouragement of the expression of feelings, informal corporate structures and relationships engaged in by the leader to increase support and commitment to corporate policies and goals.

Developing Trust through the Helping Relationship

We can summarize the main elements of the helping relationship as one in which we look at other people in terms of their potential. It is evaluation-free. Leaders who are judgmental may find few opportunities to provide real, needed help to followers. They may also find that by judging they trade off trust. By acting sensitively, helping leaders avoid becoming a threat. They accept other people as they are. Helping leaders do not try to change others; instead, they appreciate their uniqueness. Helping leaders also display attitudes of warmth, caring, liking, respect and interest towards followers. They try to see things as the other person sees them. They relate on both an objective *and* a feeling level.

Developing Trust through Active Listening

Active listening is a process that asks the listener to get inside the speaker and understand his or her point of view. It is listening for total meaning and involves listening for content and feelings, not just for content. It is a kind of naive listening (Fairholm, 1991) where the listener listens as if he or she has never heard the communicated information before.

Developing Trust through a Consistent Leadership Style

The impetus in developing trust is toward a consistent style. Leaders can use any style of leadership to encourage trust, but the essential need is for consistency in applying that style. As followers come to rely on the leader to behave in a consistent and predictable way, they can be free to extend their trust to that leader. When behavior is erratic, there is no true foundation upon which to develop trust.

LEADERSHIP OF THE TRUST CULTURE

The job of the leader is to leave no doubt in the minds of followers and others as to exactly what the organization's priorities and tasks are. This role places two obligations on leaders. The first is to create a common culture where all members can trust one another to do their part to attain agreed-upon results. The second is to insure that the trust culture created allows individual members to grow toward their personal self-development goals.

Culture setting is a value-displacement activity. Leaders engage in action to explicitly alter specific values and common behaviors. Culture leadership is one of the major activities of leaders. It forms and maintains the group. When someone joins an organization, that organization's values eventually take precedence over the individual's values. These new values prescribe the member's subsequent behavior in that group. That is why the management of corporate culture is so important a tool for the leader. If the leader doesn't shape the culture, someone else will, who will have different motives and desire different results.

The recent literature on leadership is redefining the concept. Leadership means paying attention to a few important (to the leader) programs, values, ideas and ideals. This focusing provides a professional and psychological direction, a value base and a system of balancing competing ideas, values and systems in the culture. Leaders use symbols, ideas, words, objects, processes or other objects or ideas reflecting aspects of corporate culture. Leaders also set corporate standards; they teach them, live them and inspire others to live them.

Team Building

A team is a group of people who share a common purpose and work in a coordinated and interdependent relationship. Teams help members create a positive culture; one identified by high-trust levels. Team relationships allow members to align with the culture and the team's purposes. They lead to synergy.

Team participation engages the mental and emotional involvement of leaders and followers: that is, the involvement of the member's egos as well as their physical and mental capacities. Teaming also asks members to exercise their creative self and to increase their personal sense of responsibility through involvement. Team members need to recognize that the corporation wants their total involvement. And, when given, involvement increases the member's sense of responsibility and ownership for the corporation and its results.

Adair (1986) says that teamwork is the byproduct of empowering leadership. Team leaders are members of teams, not outside the team. Teams do not emphasize normal rules of authority and hierarchy, though the leader may legally have the last word. Rather, consultation in which leaders have a high degree of self-confidence is part of leading teams.

Team leadership requires different skills of the leader, not the least of which is the ability to share power. Communications are also critical in team leadership as are skills in value displacement. Choosing the right people to be on the team is also critical to team success. Members need to be technically competent, have an ability to work with others and have desirable personal attitudes.

Familiarity with team members, however, may interfere with a leader's ability to be impartial. Team building is a slow process. It consumes a lot of the leader's energy. Becoming familiar with team members and their way of thinking and behaving may make it easier to set and meet high standards. Without top-level support, team leadership methods may be frustrated.

Empowerment

Today's work force is typically better educated and far more independent than formerly. Workers are aware and wanting. Pfeffer (1981) says that people want to achieve control over their environment. Many suggest that survival in the future is dependent on more empowered, self-directed workers. Empowering followers also enhances and strengthens leaders. Leaders are coming to recognize this and changing their behavior to share power with coworkers.

Many leaders routinely engage in empowering technologies. In helping followers to develop and use their talents on the job, leaders frequently use this technology. Empowerment works because it supports deep psychological needs of people in groups. People want to make a difference, and if leaders let them do so and teach them how they gain followers.

Conger and Kanungo (1988) define to empower as to "enable" rather than simply to delegate. In developing, rewarding and recognizing those around them, leaders are allowing the human assets with which they work to appreciate. The leader's actions to empower also involve sensitizing coworkers to recognize their power and capacities and training them in their full use.

Empowerment is exercising control based on results, not just activities, events or methods. Empowerment is endowing others with the power required to perform a given act. It is granting another the practical autonomy to step out and contribute directly to his or her job. It does not mean that leaders give away their power. Rather it involves adding to the power of coworkers. No one is powerless. Empowerment is sensitizing coworkers to this fact.

Empowerment is intellectually connected with several leadership ideas. Team or participative management ideas imply empowerment, although few of the original theorists identified this explicitly. Empowerment is also part of transformational leadership ideas that imply changing the individual as well as the team. Transformational leadership enables leaders and followers to reach higher levels of accomplishment and motivation. McGregor's (1960) Theory Y is another intellectual foundation of empowerment. People who fundamentally believe that others are good and want to work and accept responsibility will empower their followers with the opportunity to use these capacities.

There is some risk inherent in empowerment of others. It requires the leader to have faith in the essential goodness of followers. Leaders need to trust in the talent, commitment and capacity of followers to work independently and to develop new ways to do the work. This is a very different virtual environment than that of traditional leadership or management contexts.

Inspiration

To inspire means to enliven, excite or animate another person. It is akin to motivation, in that when we feel inspired we want to act on that feeling. But inspiration goes beyond motivation in appealing to a need to be part of, and engaged with others in, a lofty enterprise. It is a particular relationship between an individual and a leader.

To inspire someone the leader must appeal to them on a different level than internal drives. Inspiration is more than rational. It is extra-rational. It appeals to the emotions, to the spiritual self, to the super-natural dimensions of personality. People inspire us when they take us outside (beyond) our routine ways of thinking and behaving and lead us to another, higher, reality.

Inspiration implies several ideas. *First*, it involves a confirmation in the heart of the believer that the common message (vision) of the team is true. *Second*, it connotes the idea of guidance to the individual be-liever in his or her group relationships. *Third*, inspiration is a means to fully understand the inspiring vision. *Fourth*, inspirational messages are a way for the believer to have communion with other believers. *Fifth*, it impels one to do good, to strive for excellence. *Sixth*, it carries with it a feeling of rightness. And, *finally*, inspiration has a teaching component. It is a way to teach others, a method of teaching.

Inspirational action or words by the leader are inspiring because they clarify and vivify what is already in the hearts of followers. The reason we call the leader's vision a vision is that leaders put in words the hopes and dreams of followers; but the dreams are already in their hearts. Visions become inspiring because of this and because leaders have touched powerful inner emotions and desires shared by others in the organization.

Quality

Improving process or output quality involves the leader in altering culture since improvements in working conditions, job design and work-ing environment have a profound impact on the employees' attitudes and actions. The quality movement dictates that we pay close attention to products and services, as well as processes, procedures and infor-mation. Organizational quality requires a new virtual environment, a new way for everyone to think about and do his or her job.

Innovation

Innovation is a hallmark of leadership. Innovation is necessary to progress. It requires a willingness to take the risk of failure or loss. Innovation is experimentation. Leaders are especially adroit at re-sponding to change of any sort. Innovation defines leaders. They use innovation to try to change the corporation to fit the world. Managers often try to change the world to match the organization.

Ownership

Ownership refers to the feelings workers have of being responsible for, of owning, the organization. It comes from being in charge, from having control over one's own work situations. It is a way to describe commitment, but it goes beyond commitment. Owners typically perform at a higher level of quality than do workers or employees. Ownership turns employees on. To foster it, leaders must allow employees some control over their work situation and keep them continuously informed about the status, problems and potential of the corporation.

Owners make decisions that affect their life and their team in real ways. Fostering ownership is a key leader task. Ownership implies that every employee is a manager (Myers, 1970). Fostering ownership usually requires leaders create small problem-solving teams and to insure that information goes to as wide an audience as possible. Leading worker-owners changes the way leaders deal with followers. They seek solutions from as low in the team as possible. They allow coworkers enough resources to do their job their own way. They do not overcontrol.

Leaders who foster feelings of ownership in followers decentralize as much as possible. They delegate to the limit of their authority and good sense. Such leaders create other leaders out of followers at several levels in the organization. They create a climate of personal satisfaction, individual dignity, challenge and opportunity to be successful. Allowing others to share ownership feelings about the group, its work process and products provides all with a stake in the outcome. It creates a sense of individual and corporate worth.

RESULTS OF TRUST LEADERSHIP

Several outcomes can be listed that result from the leadership of trust cultures. They represent significant new activities for leaders. They also define new ways to measure performance.

Shared Governance

Shared governance is a genuine sharing of the power to plan and decide with staff. The basic assumption is that this collaborative effort between management and worker will increase satisfaction and performance. In essence shared governance involves creating worker governing bodies or councils to flatten the structural hierarchy and bring decision making closer to the workers. This is a culture-creation task. The idea is to include workers in forums that are specifically created to share planning and decision making at the lowest corporate levels.

Shared governance emphasizes the importance of broadly defusing information. It honors and values the individual. It is built on the idea that when group and individual values are congruent, more productivity and satisfaction result (Jernigan, 1997). It places responsibility for corporate success equally on both leaders and workers.

This idea of shared governance permeates the trust-leadership virtual environment. Shared governance asks leaders to collaborate with workers. It focuses the leader's work ethic on follower growth and is the essence of the relationship between them and their followers. It is a process of educating coworkers to take more control over their work lives. It is empowering them to take personal responsibility for the organization's goals and work process by including them in decisions that affect worker's actions.

Leadership in today's world is changing. To be successful the leader must be willing to engage in a continuing program of personal mental, attitudinal and behavior change to develop those capacities and those values that honor both people and high-quality performance at all levels. Leaders must assimilate these values into their personal professional lives in all their decisions and actions. And they must ignite an equal concern in workers for their growth and transformation so they will want to use more of their innate talent and intelligence in doing the organization's work.

Trust Building

As noted, trust is central to any continuing relationship. A study by Merta Martin (1996) developed the idea that leadership is a function of trust. Her findings show a high correlation between the followers' perceptions of their leader's action to set a vision and develop a trust culture and their willingness to respond as the leader desires. While both evolving a vision and fostering trust are important in leadership success in getting followers to behave as the leaders desire, developing trust is statistically more significant ($r = .84$, $p = .000$ for trust and $r = .81$, $p = .000$ for vision). When both are present in the culture, the correlation with the followers' behaviors is strongest ($r = .88$, $p = .000$).

Martin's work (using over 4,500 practicing executives) concludes that basing leadership on both (or either) trust and vision results in behavior from followers that is congruent with the leader's desires. Conversely, undesirable results can be expected if trust is lacking or the vision is unclear or ambiguous. She found her results to be consistent even when correlated with the demographic factors of age, sex or length of service as a leader.

Culture Building

Recent research by Robert Colvin (1996) suggests that culture-focused leader actions can also be very effective in influencing followers in desired ways. He concluded that there is a strong positive correlation between leader behavior that emphasizes building and maintaining a compatible culture and attaining desired responses from followers. He defines culture-focused activities as, among other things, fostering a common vision, establishing and using common values, linking team action to the broader organization, clarifying mission and strategic choices and championing initiatives beyond the narrow scope of the work. Colvin concludes that building and maintaining a cultural environment consistent with vision values results in leader success.

Colvin also coupled culture-focused action with leader action to focus on the individual in the group. These actions include teaching, coaching, mentoring and empowering workers. In concert with culture building, leader actions that focus on both culture building and the individual concerns of followers achieve the most dramatic results from followers. Colvin's research findings are statistically significant for both the leader's culture-building actions ($r = .84$, $p = .000$) and his or her individual-focused behavior ($r = .92$, $p = .000$). Either leadership approach is effective; however, individual-focused actions are, statistically, a little more significant. But, when leaders exhibit both behaviors simultaneously, their expectations for desired responses from followers are most assured.

14

Leadership and Multiculturalism

Creating and maintaining a corporate culture conducive of high trust is becoming more difficult today. The character of our work force is changing: becoming more diverse and less harmonious. The people coming into our organizations enter with different values, mores and customs. These cultural differences in the people making up the American corporation pose major problems in developing a trust culture. Indeed, diversity itself makes the task of developing leadership more difficult.

The leader's role is to build unity, a team, out of different individuals. We distinguish leaders by the fact that they provide the values and the vision around which group consensus can be sought. Leaders can lead only united, compatible colleagues who, in essence, volunteer to accept the leader's values and methods. This is contrary to the prevalent view that a consensus-seeking process can ascertain vision and values.

Common visions and values result from articulation by one person of ideals that the larger group can come to accept and around which they can coalesce. It is not a function of amalgamation, but of reduction to the core essence. The growing diversity in the workplace challenges the leader's ability to lead at all unless he or she can induce increasingly diverse people to accept common values, one vision and similar perspectives.

SAMENESS AMID DIVERSITY

Some conclude that unrestrained acceptance of all other cultures is desirable, a goal leaders should actively seek. On the surface, this idea is attractive. After all, who wants to be bigoted? But, significantly, the literature extolling cultural equality largely ignores the costs of uncontrolled enthusiasm in this regard. For our purposes, the sense of the discussion thus far in this book is that a key cost of acceptance of full diversity is the loss of the very capacity of leaders to lead. Trust and diversity for diversity's sake do not constitute a viable formula. Effective leadership in diverse organizations is simply not possible.

Fortunately, the leader's task in leading in this increasingly diverse world is not as daunting as it may first appear. Of course increasingly dissimilar kinds of people are entering the work force and demanding different treatment. But some underlying forces are also present in the American workforce, pushing toward needed unity.

While the existence of more cultural differences is a fact in our organizations and in the general culture, there is also a traditional culture already present. Our corporations are really subcultures of an identifiable and strong national culture. This cultural foundation forms a viable base for mutual action, trust and support. It can help corporate leaders build unity in their work teams.

Cultural relativists reject the idea that any culture is better in any way than another. The effect of this virtual environment is to accept all people's values and their resultant behavior, whether or not they thwart necessary group action like productivity. The unbiased facts lead to the conclusion that unrestrained cultural relativism leads to disaster. Leadership, on the other hand, is an integrative activity that proposes one value system, one culture, around which many people can gather to accomplish socially useful results.

There are too many cultures that condoned slavery, the subjugation of women and children and other human degradations to let us conclude that all cultures are equally good. Of course all cultures include some attractive cultural features. Leaders need to exercise discretion in selecting which features to use. The leader's job is to accept the good and reject values and behavior that are undesirable.

Many cultures include values, ideals or behavior that work against effective, coordinated performance. For example, American society typically does not accept cultural values that regard punctuality as unimportant or that condone nepotism; nor does it condone bribery, child labor or a host of other determined values or behaviors. These examples of unacceptable values are inimical to efficient interpersonal relationships. We normally do not accept them. We do not value them equally with values like cooperation, hard work and the effective use of time. The leader's job is to create a new value system that supersedes inappropriate ones introduced into the corporation by diverse people.

Of course all Americans should be open to new values and alternative ways to behave. But we need to match these alternative prospects with what we have now and only change when we are sure the change will add to civilization. New visions and values should not take us away from clear corporate or societal goals, whether or not they are politically correct. Leaders are in the vanguard of this change. They direct it, shape new cultures and redefine the acceptable within their social groups and corporations and for their willing followers.

As noted, the values of the people in these diverse subcultures differ widely. Each displays, even heralds, unique cultural customs. Leaders in culturally diverse groups have the difficult task to maintain as much of the diversity found in their workers as possible. They also have an equally important task of molding these diverse values and customs into a new and different culture, one that asks members to trust one another and cooperate according to specific leader-set corporate values.

The task is to unify, even homogenize, disparate coworkers with mismatched cultural values. Adherence to these sometimes new unifying corporate cultural values may require that team members follow even at the cost of reducing full adherence to some of their formerly cherished values. But this has always been a requirement of membership. Members of any group are distinguished by their acceptance of a specific set of standards and rules of conduct to the exclusion of all others.

Each culture represented in the work force, and in the larger community within which the corporation operates, reflects cultural values that, while often including similar values, attach different levels of importance to each. Each corporation's unique cultural value mix represents a challenge to leaders.

Diversity places increased pressure on leaders. Different people have different needs. To foster excellent performance, leaders must accommodate these needs. Complicating the situation even more, these needs change in the individual over time. The leader's task is one of continually building homogenous work groups within which leadership can take place. This task is even more important in these times of multiple changes.

LEADING A CULTURALLY DIVERSE WORK FORCE

Leaders will have to learn to lead work forces that are continually changing. They will have to be more effective in working with superiors, peers and subordinates. They will also have to meet the needs of clients, customers, suppliers and the average citizen, all of whom may differ from themselves. And, they will need to keep their focus on progress, innovation and excellence.

The challenge is great, but the benefits can be enormous. They may include a more open corporate culture. Better business decisions may result from a group with more diverse experiences. There can be more responsiveness to diverse customers. The corporation may become more loyal, as workers feel they are valued for themselves, not just for their skills or labor. And, the team may enjoy a competitive advantage since they can make use of this new, different and expanded labor pool.

Leading culturally diverse workers is not an exercise in mere acceptance. It is an exercise in creativity. The leader's task is to create a new culture and new values to which we can induce diverse people to conform for their own benefit and that of the organization. Leading culturally diverse workers asks the leader to be culturally creative, not culturally inclusive.

Leaders who are more culturally sensitive will be better able to understand and serve their customers and all stakeholders. This benefits the diverse corporation over its less differentiated competitors. An individual's performance and career advancement often depend on working relationships with others. As the "others" become more dissimilar, all members of our organizations must become more sensitive to cultural factors and to the culturally-based actions of their coworkers.

Leaders need to develop skills in accepting and using different people and methods to add to the organization's capacity to survive in a growing and increasingly complex world. They also need to suppress their feelings of fear and antagonism and increase their capacity to accept differences. And, they need to be proactive in seeking leadership training in situations of cultural diversity.

LEADING FOR CULTURAL UNITY, NOT DIVERSITY

As more people are entering the workplace with different cultural backgrounds, the pressure is on the corporate culture to change. Established business expectations, rites and rituals will have to be altered for the new but different worker; and some of the present cultural systems may need to be discarded.

The goals for leaders are still the same, however. The leadership role in leading a diverse work force is first to define common values and customs. The second role is to integrate and acculturate workers into the team culture, its value systems and operating practices. The process is to set a vision, seek consensus on that vision and then legitimize that vision throughout the culture.

Leading in a diverse culture is complicated. Leaders must manage a variety of internal and external forces and operating systems to be effective. Managing culture to develop interpersonal trust is fundamentally a task of value change. The change needed is to match worker performance with organizational need while resolving a variety of operating system problems. The organization's system of communications is one example.

Managing communication systems is really managing meanings. When leaders translate verbal and written materials into understandable values, purposes, policies and procedures, they are managing a cultural feature as well as the technical system of information flow. Unless workers perceive the information flowing to them as appropriate, useful and "right" for them, the mechanical process of passing information to them will be sterile and useless.

Similarly, corporate training programs are as much culture-creation opportunities as simple skills-building ones. Whether the training program concentrates on job-related skills building, corporate philosophy, remedial reading and writing, English as a second language or problem-solving skills, the goals sought must also include the transfer of ideology, values and context. Without these cultural features the training will not be complete, nor can we expect it to fully serve the corporation's needs.

These examples are typical of situations many leaders face in their work. They are cultural more than technical problems. They ask leaders to create culturally harmonious teams. It is a process of integration of workers into teams, not factions.

Cultural factionalism in the team costs leaders time and resources. Dealing with special interests and advocacy groups and responding to charges of bias or favoritism can take considerable time and resources. Organizational factionalism also contributes to lost time in directing a diverse work force that does not respond equally to an instruction or order or policy. Poor morale is also a frequent result that contributes to a loss of productivity.

Unfettered corporate factionalism that some say reduces bias may, in fact, produce more conflict based on bigotry. For example, as we allow members of corporate subcultures to behave in non-conforming ways or receive different treatment, we can expect those not similarly treated to react in non-helpful ways. High trust cannot exist in this kind of situation, nor can high quality, productivity or long-term corporate excellence.

Leaders need to give attention to setting work and accountability standards that consider the diverse nature of their work force. They also need to be willing to alter these standards as the situation demands. These standards should be reflected in corporate design—for example, in shared responsibility teams, matrix organizations or Quality Circles. The culturally responsive corporation will embody appropriate job standards in job structure and content. It will merge them in position descriptions that reflect the interchangeability of skills; and in work schedules that provide for flex time, job sharing and other flexible employment systems. These standards become the means to allocate authority and encourage employee involvement and participation.

OBSTACLES TO SHAPING TRUST CULTURES

A trust culture is a complex structure composed of people in informal and formal relationships, work processes, physical facilities and reflected in institutional goals. Failure in any of these subsystems can affect the whole. Unfortunately failures in corporate systems can happen when we do too much of the right thing as well as when we do too little.

Some corporate barriers to creating or maintaining an effective trust culture flow out of these overreactions. Berkley (1984) suggests that we hamper development of an effective trust culture when the corporation or one of its components survives beyond its normal effective life. We also hamper the development of effective trust cultures when traditional behavior patterns dominate the need for change. This is also the case when the corporate tendency to bigness becomes counterproductive. Trust cultures also suffer when some corporate components seek status vis-à-vis their peers.

Leaders also need to be wary of the dynamics of male-female relationships. They should be cautious of sexist stereotypes carried over from their earlier experiences. Many leaders carry fuzzy distinctions in their minds about romance and harassment. Most leaders need training in how to handle office romance. But, because of the newness of this phenomenon and the complexity of direct action, expecting training in the management of office romances to be a cure-all is unrealistic. Creating and shaping a culture that considers the potentiality of office romance in the firm is a more effective and longer—term strategy. The task is to accommodate this prospect within an overall culture of mutual support, encouragement and opportunity for individual improvement and collective success.

PART V

The Spiritual Heart of Leadership

Our understanding of leadership has made another shift to a final virtual environment in preparation for the twenty-first century. It builds on the idea that leadership is a function of values-and-trust-culture maintenance. The center of attention now is on the basic nature of the individual: that is, the spiritual nature, of both the leader and the led. This virtual environment asks leaders to see each worker as a whole person with a variety of skills, knowledge and abilities that invariably go beyond the narrow confines of job needs.

Spirituality is a new notion in leadership. We have ignored this idea for most of the 100-year history of modern leadership theory. Spiritualilty is not even mentioned in contemporary textbooks. Yet, throughout all of social history we have listed inner moral—spiritual—standards as the primary influence of human action. Our sense of spirit defines humankind, determines our guiding values and directs our most intimate and important choices and actions. To leave it out of our thinking about leadership is to diminish, perhaps to irrelevance, our theory and unnecessarily constrain our potential success.

15

The Place of Spirit in Our Work Lives

Our inner self has a powerful life of its own. It controls both individual and collective action. As we advance in our understanding of the nature of work, workers and leadership, we must also advance in our understanding of the spiritual dimension of these ideas. It is clearly necessary to invent corporate forms appropriate to the multicultural, electronic, global age. But we doom such efforts to failure if they do not respond to something deeper. They must reflect the widely held core values of the participants.

The present attention given to the spiritual self in leadership thinking is, in part, a reflection of the increased importance given to work in the lives of most people. Work has become the center of our lives. Whether we like it or not, work is becoming the source of values in our society and the site of our most worthwhile contributions. The work community has become our most significant community, and the workplace is fast becoming the place where most of us find our sense of full meaning.

It is hard for many of us to separate our work from the rest of our life. Obviously it is central to economic well-being. It is also central to personal and group happiness. Given the dominance of our work lives, if personal, professional or social transformation is to take place, it will most likely take place at work. For after all, life is about spirit. We humans have only one spirit, which must manifest itself in both our personal and professional lives.

People in all kinds of occupations are voicing a cry for spiritual foundation in a chaotic world. They are redefining work to include satisfaction of the inner needs for spiritual identity and satisfaction. Jacobson's (1995) survey of national leaders and the author's survey of mid-level managers (Fairholm, 1997) confirm a growing need for workplace cultures, leadership and work processes that celebrate the whole individual with needs, desires, values and a "wanting" spirit self. These studies provide verification of the presence today—and always—of spiritual forces in the workplace.

These and other studies document the pressure we feel to recognize and respond to the sacred in us. Our spiritual self is finding outlet in the secular workplace. It is no longer the case, if it ever was, that production alone defines successful leadership. Leaders bring their whole self to the work of leadership. They must, and many do, include their knowledge of the spiritual dimension of life that, perhaps more powerfully than any other force, shapes human action over the long term.

Of course, detailed knowledge about system, process and procedures is important, but knowledge about our own and our followers' spiritual side is essential. Spirit is about what we are. It is who we are, and why we think we are here in life, that ultimately guides our behavior. Our spiritual dimension conditions our relationships with others and their relationships with us. The idea of spirit is central to life. It is also central to any activity like leadership that purports to order and direct our human condition.

The change to give attention to this virtual environment is only now taking place. It introduces another powerful drive coming not just from the few people at the head of the business hierarchy, but also from ordinary workers. It is a drive to become all that they can become within the confines of the corporate work unit. Spiritual leadership is a reflection of a rising worker demand for the opportunity to use and hone more of their skills and abilities than just those used on the assembly line or prescribed by confining standard operating procedures. It is simply not possible to attain success today and to establish and maintain corporate health and vigor without considering both the needs and desires of workers.

The reasons for this reoriented leader mind-set are many. They reflect major changes in our social undergirding and have been abundantly addressed in recent years. Among them the rise of an increasingly diverse labor pool made up of workers, each with different kinds of experiences and striving to honor different core values systems, seems particularly cogent. Changes in the nature of the work done today are also key. Today most workers are knowledge workers, people who use words and numbers as both the raw material and the results of their work effort.

The rise of knowledge work has changed the workplace into what

Senge (1990) has called the learning organization, a workplace characterized by continuous worker growth and development to keep up with ever changing customer demands for unique products and services. Today's workers want and expect the firm to provide them with the kinds of work and satisfactions that former generations of workers expected to receive only after years of work and promotion to supervisory ranks (Myers, 1970).

A spiritual core lies at the heart of all human life. It expresses itself in beauty, aesthetics and in our relationships with others (Jacobs, 1994). We need to reconnect to the fact that our hearts and minds, and not just our bodies, are dominant in our business relationships. For life is about spirit, and we humans carry only one spirit that manifests itself in both our life and our livelihood.

SPIRITUALITY AND WORK

For most of human history no one had to search for the sacred. At the core of every culture was a cult, with sacred times and places set aside for public rituals. For most of our history religion was the core force that created our sense of morality, of right and wrong. Religious principles defined moral conduct. They defined good and evil and provided the context for human interactivity.

Today it is otherwise. Now we move in a secular time and space. We have lost our religious moral roots. In a drive for so-called sophistication, many people have dropped their dedication to a specific religious orthodoxy. Instead, many of us are looking for the sacred from what we do every day, our work. Work is the place where we spend most of our time and to which we devote most of our true selves. It is logical that we should seek a secular substitute for our lost morality in our workplace, the place where we occupy ourselves most fully and through which we define ourselves.

Spirituality is the essence of who we are. It is about our inner self, separate from the body. It includes the way we think and the thoughts we think, as well as our perceptions of the world. Often it has some religious overtones.[1] But, spirituality is also about our inner or private being, our real self. It is evident in social, emotional and intellectual activities. It transcends normal physical and biological wants and needs. For many, spirituality is the intangible, life-giving force in all people, a state of intimate relationship with the inner world of higher values and morality (Vaill, 1989).

[1]While important, the religious nature of spirituality is not considered here. This aspect of spirituality is better accommodated in doctrinaire religions and their social instrumentalities. Indeed, many, including this author, would object to matters of personal religion being introduced in the workplace.

Few will accept this easily, but what is most needed today is not more intellect, but more soul (Boyce, 1995). Neglect of our spiritual nature helps explain the whole range of workplace problems we now face—the persistence of hopelessness, worker anomie, lowered productivity and substance abuse (Raspberry, 1995). Efforts aimed at improving people's lives that don't have a moral and spiritual dimension are literally a waste of time. A sense of spirituality is the anchor for most people's work ethics and social morality (Range, 1995).

The idea of spirit at work is in reality a shift in our virtual environment. In the past it was easy to compartmentalize our mind so that each part of our life competed for its own self-interests in relationship to all others. The tendency now is to view life and living as a vast number of cooperative relationships with other independent units. In terms of our work, this is nothing less than a total reinvention of the workplace, a redefinition of work as not merely an economic site, but a prime locus of life. Nevertheless, current efforts to reinvent work ignore the human element.

An implicit acknowledgment of the need to recognize the spiritual side of our work lives should be at the heart of the current talk about reinventing work, not merely downsizing, efficiency or flexibility. This kind of spiritual focus starts with a personal context. It asks leaders to orchestrate a new personal context among group members. Adding a spiritual element can produce meaningful change (Goss, Pascale and Athos, 1994).

Leadership is coming to mean the task of creating an arena in which competing interests come together and through negotiation strike a deal with workers, as long as that deal does not intrude on what the corporation stands for. The challenge to leaders is to find a new language of the spirit, one that gives point and meaning to our lives, and then use that language to shape the corporation, our leadership of it and our concept of leadership. This is because the organization, re-shaped though it will be, will remain the lynchpin of our lives (Handy, 1994).

Badaracco and Ellsworth's research (1992) on the chief executives of several large firms confirmed what many suspect. They found that leaders are motivated by self-interest and by a search for power and wealth in the face of self-interested behavior by others. However, they also confirmed that these forces fail to fully explain the motivation of the high-caliber individuals they sought for their corporations. They found an acute need for people in leadership positions to be examples of the highest moral principles.

Being models of management efficiency is not enough. It is important that leaders have the right goals for their relationships with their followers. It is equally important that leaders employ spiritually-based forces in their relationships with followers. Success in leading on the basis of spirit is conditioned by the presence among both leaders and followers of interactive trust and shared ideals, customs and standards: in other words, by a mutually accepted cultural morality. The task of the leader is to first create this culture and then foster its values and customs among followers. Shared culture is the basis of leadership. Indeed, leadership is impossible outside a shared culture (Schein, 1985; Fairholm, 1994b).

THE NEED FOR SPIRITUAL LEADERSHIP

Leaders share their leadership tasks with their core of workers and other officers as they work together to provide the climate and conditions within which both leader and led can strive for excellence. This striving is personal for the individual leader. It also asks leaders to encourage followers to want to strive for personal excellence themselves. Spiritual leadership helps followers by empowering them to similar service. This leadership is also directed toward maintaining a climate to help followers freely accept the challenge to excellence. Conformity may bring unity, but it also often brings mediocrity.

There is necessarily some leader and some manager in each of us. The problem is one of a proper balance of these skills in ourself and the organizations we serve. Unfortunately today, in too many people and organizations, the manager predominates—to the virtual exclusion of leadership. The cause can largely be traced to the simplicity and comfort of measurement and control, the central facets of management today. Simply put, it is easier—not necessarily better—to manage than to lead.

Leadership, in contrast to management, places a higher emphasis on values: on creativity, intelligence, integrity. Unfortunately, these are the same values and traits managers seek to screen out in interviews in favor of loyalty, conformity and unit cohesion. But it is precisely these qualities that are most needed today. Our corporations and their members cry out for interesting, exciting, challenging work and leaders who can make the work seem worth our personal time and identity.

Spiritual leaders provide this. They add values to system and technique. Value-oriented spiritual leaders often work within existing situations and resources to leverage assets and outcomes beyond expectations (Myers, 1993). They ratchet performance up by displaying distinctive leadership in relationships with others. They open up avenues of awareness and choice. They focus the team they lead to exciting visions. They integrate diverse perspectives and action patterns, and they add innovation to performance. They are infectious self-starters who tend to influence others in the work environment with their spirit and enthusiasm. They keep the corporation sharp by raising the awareness of problems and opportunities.

We have obviously reached a point where non-intuitive, leaner, rational management has made a mess of American companies. We badly need true leaders who have a belief in the value of what they do and in the collective vision and mission. Numerical surrogates for reality do not begin to take account of the rhythms of life or the rich dynamics of the human spirit. The true leader can see situations in different ways and then bring these alternatives to consciousness so other people can appreciate and act on them. They get beyond spreadsheet analysis to the essence of these situations, to their spirituality.

Spirituality is standing for something bigger than self that others can also believe in. That is also leadership. Obviously, the individual's inner spiritual self is, and has always been, a part of his interactions with others. It has only very recently entered the arena of academic and practitioner conversation. An understanding of the spiritual side of leadership must include recognizing the spirit in self and others and the spiritual basis of interpersonal connections.

16

Defining Spiritual Leadership

The spiritual in us describes the animating or life-giving principle within a human being or in an event or thing. It is the part of the human being we associate with the mind or feelings as distinguished from the physical body. We can define the idea of the spiritual as the essential human values from around the world and across time that teach us how humanity belongs within the greater scheme of circumstances and how we can realize harmony in our life and work (Heerman, 1995).

Secular and spiritual are not opposed, because we need not limit the spiritual to a religious context. Traditional religion is still the prime repository of moral history and present practice. For many it is the context within which moral virtues are defined and the standard of the moral life. Nothing said here is intended to diminish this idea. Rather, the attempt is only to underline the importance of religious and moral values in directing our individual lives and to suggest that, as society or individuals move away from traditional religion, they still must find an outlet for these moral drives. For a growing number of people, that outlet is in the work they do.

Our spirituality is a source guide for personal values and for the meaning we give to life. It is a way of understanding our own world, an inner awareness. It is a means of integration of the self and the world (Jacobson, 1995). Spirituality is another word for personal awareness. It is the acceptance of universal values that individuals believe guide their everyday actions and by which they judge their own actions. Spirituality in the corporation refers to the inner values of the

leader and the followers—the mature principles, qualities and influences that we implicitly exhibit in our behavior and interactions with
other people.

Integrating the many components of one's work and personal life into
a comprehensive system for managing the workplace defines the holistic or spiritual leadership approach. It provides the platform for leadership that recognizes this spiritual element in people and in their
behavior. This new holistic approach will help companies realize a mul-
titude of significant benefits. By using a comprehensive holistic approach, they can focus their investments of people, money, time and
resources to get the maximum return possible (Kuritz, 1992).

FOUNDATIONS OF SPIRITUAL LEADERSHIP

The spiritual-leadership virtual environment sees the transformation of self, others and the team as important, even critical. This new
leadership reality is that of the servant leader. This model values the
education, inspiration and development of others. To function in this
way, leaders need a change of heart—of spirit—not just technique. The
model of spiritual leadership asks leaders to put those they serve first
and let everything else take care of itself.

Leaders are first servants of those they lead. They are teachers,
sources of information and knowledge and standard setters more than
givers of directions or disciplinarians. This leadership environment is
radically different from the non-leadership managerial virtual environment and more rudimentary earlier leadership virtual environments.
On the surface at least, it is counter to conventional wisdom. The difference is not one of quantity, but of quality. It represents a mind shift.
Spirituality stretches the leader's mind toward vision, toward reality,
toward courage, toward ethics. It accepts much of the context of values-
based leadership. But the spiritual-leadership virtual environment lets
us add timeless issues of the spirit to the formula for leadership success.

Popular culture celebrates the material and largely ignores the spirit.
But competition and compassion need not be mutually exclusive. Indeed, for many people, the goal of work may ultimately be to more
deeply become people of quality. The biggest mistake of current leadership texts is that they confuse dedication, mission and vision with
spirituality. People are looking for significance in their work and the
opportunity to use their minds and feelings in concert with the energizing life-giving principles within them.

Traditionally, leadership has been defined in terms of the institutional head: the person or small group who provides method and direction to the organization. Knowing which rule to follow, which tool to
use, can help us attain success in a given situation. This knowledge is

important. But it is only a part of the task of the leader. Just getting the work done and reporting in a timely manner—difficult as this sometimes is—is not all that is required.

The heart or spirit of leadership has to do with what individual leaders believe, value, dream: what they are focused on, and committed to, at an intimate level. It is about the leader's personal and institutional vision for the team and what each follower's place in it is. The leader's role in focusing team energy and commitment is more critical to group success then managerial control.

Our vision, translated to the corporate team, defines its unique place in the larger communities of work and social life. The leader's vision defines his or her spiritual focus. It reflects his or her heartfelt values. Spiritual leadership is trying to teach followers this spiritual nucleus and convince them of its utility for themselves and for other stakeholders.

The virtual environment of spiritual leadership is shaped and focused by these heartfelt values, by the leader's soul. The soul drives what we do. When we leaders respond to the values of our heart, others will know what we are truly about and can more freely choose to follow us. Only then, can the team's collective needs be met: whether individual members' needs or our own. That is, a leader's core philosophy about life and leadership is given substance and meaning by an internal system of spiritual values. These values become a vitalizing vision of the possible for the leader, followers and the team.

Seeking focus—a vision—for the team is fundamentally a decision of the heart, a commitment. Actions to demonstrate that heart-thought follow only as followers also accept this virtual environment. The mindset we accept (our heart-thoughts) defines what is for each person. It shapes and controls what our particular world-view is like. We behave according to that meaning. Together the heart and mind (our spiritual values and our intellectual skills) shape our behavior—our decisions, actions and relationships.

DEFINITIONAL ELEMENTS OF SPIRITUAL LEADERSHIP

Our spirituality defines the inner self, separate from the body, but including the physical and intellectual self. It includes the way people think and the thoughts they feel. It is a part of their overall perception of the world. Spirituality has some religious versus secular overtones, but it primarily has to do with our inner or private being, our "life-force," whether or not we see it in religious terms. Spirituality is the essence that separates mankind from all other creatures. It is manifested in emotional or intellectual activities or thoughts that transcend normal physical and biological wants or needs.

Many perceive spirituality to include a much broader range of experience, while they see religion and faith as limiting the discussion to experiences that arise in traditional institutions or ways of thinking (Vaill, 1989). Following are seven elements of a definition of spirituality taken from the author's previous research (Fairholm, 1997). The order in which each item is shown identifies the relative frequency with which it was mentioned by surveyed managers in defining and describing their conceptions of spirituality.

An Inner Certainty

For many people spirituality is the inner conviction that certain principles or beliefs are intangible and may not rest on logical proof yet are trustworthy and valuable. It is the belief that people guide their actions by a higher power with whom they have a relationship. This idea has strong religious overtones.

The idea of spirituality also describes a more secular definition of the essence of the person. Many people define spirituality as the acceptance of universal values that they believe guide their everyday actions and by which others should judge their actions.

The Essence of Self

People also define spirituality as the capacity that separates human beings from all other creatures. It refers to an inner awareness that makes integration of the self and world possible. Defined in this way, understanding spirituality is critical to understanding corporate life and leadership.

Jacobson (1995) concluded that spirituality is important and meaningful to leaders. The secular and spiritual do not have to be separate, and leaders don't separate their inner selves from the roles they play. Instead they are indivisible. This is a holistic view of leadership action, one more responsive to both our needs and our objective experience.

The Basis of Comfort, Strength, Happiness

Some people also define spirituality in personal terms, but in less metaphysical ways. Human beings have values and principles; they select qualities and influences that they exhibit in their behavior and interactions with other human beings. Spirituality is the part of us that we use or rely upon for comfort, strength and happiness. It is a source of contentment, both off the job and at work.

The Source of Personal Meaning, Values, Life Purposes

For some people spirituality is any philosophy that lifts us and gives meaning to our life. It is the side of us that is searching for meaning, values, ethics and life purposes. It is the ethics we follow, the degree to which we seek to do things for the common good and to be a better person. It has to do with what we do for the betterment of all. In this dimension, spirituality is a relationship with something intangible, beyond the self.

A Personal Belief System

Still others define spirituality as a personal belief system. It is being true to one's beliefs, one's internal values and ethics. It is a goodness of mind and spirit.

An Emotional Level, a Feeling

We can also define spirituality as an emotional level, a feeling. It is how we feel emotionally in our soul.

The Experience of the Transcendent in Life

Spirituality for some also partakes of the transcendent. It is acting out in thought and deeds the experience of the transcendent in human life.

Spiritual leadership is both new and old. Like all ideas, it challenges, by its very presence in the leadership arena of ideas, all old ideas and practices. It is new in the sense that to date researchers have not considered the spiritual orientation in people as a factor in their theories of leadership, management or organization. It is also new in that many people's professional intellectual environments have excluded any sense of the unique self from their preconceptions of work, workers, managers and leaders. They have ignored its force in shaping the interactions in which these corporate actors engage. As such, introduction of spirit to the workplace is new, even alien to many.

Spirituality, however, is also old. Individuals have always been aware of, and responsive to, their spiritual center. They have fostered its growth and have often let it dominate their lives both on and off the job. But they have not found a receptive community for developing individual and team spiritual values at work. As a result, many people compartmentalize their lives into work, family, religious and social spheres and relate spirit only to religion.

Nevertheless, people are the sum of their life experiences—physical, mental and spiritual. To try to compartmentalize our inner self and core values into a complex of disparate external relationships is to invite stress, tension and dysfunction. Today, when many people are spending most of their waking lives at work or in work-related situations and activities, such a bifurcated life contributes to the social maladies that characterize contemporary American life. Some reintegration of the whole person into our leadership theory is needed.

Spiritual leadership provides that holistic, integrated virtual environment. Through their personal efforts, leaders assure that the team's value system is integrated and holistic in nature so they do not have to sacrifice values (Cound, 1987). A holistic approach includes services and programs that address both the professional and personal lives of stakeholders (Rupert, 1991; Autry, 1992).

17

Problems with the Current Situation

The idea of spirituality as a major area of leadership study makes sense intellectually. However, as we attempt to apply it we may encounter problems. Prime among these problems is the fact that spiritual matters have never formed a major part of modern leadership or management theory. The result is there is little concrete ideological support for this perception of the leader's role. Consequently, young professionals are not exposed to ideas of spirit in their professional training. Indeed, they are taught to objectify, not personalize, their professional lives.

Business success is defined in objective terms. Spiritual satisfaction and professional success are seen as separate goals, which are not attainable by the same effort. Career and material acquisition, not spiritual peace or growth, are the goals in today's work world. These goals are considered more important than individual longings for harmony, peace and satisfaction: ideals sought by all people, whether at home, in church or in the office.

These pervasive human needs are ignored in past leadership mental realities. In truth, the ideal supporting current leadership discussion is based on obsolete philosophy and obsolete science. Based on 300-year-old Newtonian science and equally ancient philosophies, traditional leadership theory is insufficient to explain and predict contemporary corporate life. Past theory is inadequate to deal with the radical change and creativity that is typical of today's business world.

Spirit as the core idea in leadership theory is a radical notion. It is contrary to accepted intellectual principles and ignores deeply held feelings. The classical model of the business firm is highly structured and focuses on control of tangible objects—products, services and people. The environment within which most people work is a bureaucratic one. While good at insuring high productivity, in yielding repeatable products, it is not geared to meeting individual human needs. Hence, introducing one's spiritual sense into the discussion of leadership is foreign to many.

Nevertheless, our spiritual self is our most accurate definition of ourselves. It determines who we are and what we do. It has to be a part of our work tasks and the goals we seek from our work. But acceptance of the spiritual side of both leader and led can be difficult given the history of separation of work and worker spirit. Some of the problems spiritual leaders encounter in introducing spirit as a legitimate part of leadership thought and action are discussed below. The intent is to introduce some of the limits on spiritual leadership in the workplace arising from traditional theory and practice.

PROBLEMS ENCOUNTERED IN LEGITIMATIZING SPIRIT IN LEADERSHIP

Spirit and Professionalism

Some suggest that attention to our spiritual side discourages education and professionalism (see, for example, Peters, 1994). They believe that it is the purpose of professional training to dispel the mists and shadows of religion and free the human mind from error and delusion. Like day and night, were either of them to gain the ascendancy the reign of the other must necessarily cease.

In fact, the purpose of education is the expansion of the soul—the body and the spirit—to the fullness of its capacity. It is a bringing forth and perfecting of all the inherent powers of the individual. True education increases the strength of our faculties. It imparts nothing more useful than discipline and development. In a very real way, all human experience is an educational process. Education is the full and uniform development of the mental, physical, moral and spiritual faculties. Education of the spirit, that is, exploration of the spiritual side of self, is a part of the workaday experiences of mankind.

Spirit and Ambition to Succeed

Americans work hard. We may live well, but we no longer live nobly. Workaholism and its handmaidens, careerism and materialism, are not only social issues. These are spiritual issues—dealing with the essence of the individual, often impoverishing all values but those of material success. The quest for success is compulsive for some. For them, nothing gets in the way of work.

Business people, however, have begun to question the deeper underlying methods and motives of their leaders (Hickman, 1989). Success has nothing to do with titles. It has everything to do with the faith, the vision and the love we bring to our work. Sound moral principle is the only sure evidence of strength, the only firm foundation of greatness and perpetuity. Where this is lacking, no one's character is strong, no nation's life can be lasting. Spiritual leadership is more than a new leadership ideal; it is a seminal mind shift.

This shift influences workers and leaders and redefines their standards of success. These new standards of measurement are taking over our measures of business success and business ethics. For example, it is perhaps the ultimate statement that the world does not own us. We are made for rest and holiness as surely as we are made for work and ambition. One road to dramatic change is the move from career dependence to career self-reliance (Waterman, 1994). Another thing we can do is to place work in its proper context. We can judge ourselves (and force others to also judge us) on a different measure: not by what we do, but by how and for what reasons we work. No matter what the work we do is, it can be done better with heart and spirit.

Spirit and Self-overcoming

The greatest problems leaders face are not the surface challenges of work, worker and product. The greatest challenges lie deep inside the leader's spirit and that of their followers. The spirit contains everything in our character we try to express because it makes us feel good, as well as everything we want to suppress because it is painful. Getting in touch with our inner spiritual being lets us inventory and use our best qualities, like confidence, quickness, alertness, dedication, courage, perseverance, charm, thriftiness, trust, commitment, faith, hope and love.

We can also define our spirit by less than positive traits. There is a hidden part of our spirit, our hidden self, the aspects of our personality that we don't like to acknowledge or that society discourages us from showing. It too is part of what makes us human. We need to bring this less attractive self to the fore of the mind occasionally for scrutiny or these negative aspects of self will turn toxic. Thinking about our negative inclinations and forming strategies to counter them is also part of sensitivity to our spiritual side.

PRESSURES THAT FOCUS OUR SPIRITUAL SELF AT WORK

Management practice has for 100 years been things-, not people-oriented. However, much of today's work is to produce information, facts and ideas. The people, the knowledge workers, creating and using these facts want involvement. They want to direct their work lives and add to their level of competence, whether or not they are in a leadership position (Myers, 1970). Current management and structural models are incompatible with this new push for worker self-determination.

Consider the following:

The Pressure of Spirit

Workers today are asking the company to weave personal, spiritual, social and environmental dimensions into the fabric of corporate work life. Business is after all simply another form of human activity. Workers are saying that we should not expect less from it than we do from other social institutions. Today's workers want their work to be more human-oriented, more humane.

The Changing Nature of Work

Plainly work is changing. No longer do we need machine-like bureaucratic procedures. Rather, the movement is from unskilled work to knowledge work, from individual work to teamwork. We are replacing meaningless, repetitive tasks, with innovative ones. We now ask our workers—and they are asking leaders—to move from a system that required of them single-skilled expertise to one requiring many skills (Pinchot and Pinchot, 1994). Power is moving away from supervisors and toward workers and customers. We are replacing coordination from above with cooperation among peers.

Demographics

There are more young, highly educated people coming to work in our corporations and social institutions today who focus on self-fulfillment values. It is logical that these values are carried into the workplace when these young people enter the job market. They are no longer willing to accept the values and expectations of their parents or of their supervisors. They see work as merely another extension of their lives, another venue to practice their own style of relationships and an additional arena where they can receive the intellectual, emotional and spiritual stimulation they want.

Changes in Social Subsystems

Changes in family structure, work cultures and society all combine to move society toward different work-related goals and methods of interpersonal relations. Downsizing, baby-boomer value shifts and technological systems improvements have created a situation where fewer workers are needed to do necessary (but changed) work. The role of the middle manager has changed. The present circumstance has produced a situation where workers often do not need supervisors very much. The constant tension resulting from accelerating change places impossible pressures on traditional structures and on workers.

New Psychological Work Contracts

The abandonment of the traditional psychological contract connecting workers to a life-long career with the company has effectively destroyed the security and tranquility of the workplace (Cappelli, 1995). People need something to repair the damage. For a growing cadre of people spirituality is the answer. Workers are voicing their hunger to include inner spiritual needs as well as economic and production needs in the work experience. They expect more from their work than just a pay check. They are asking that their values be not only considered, but also reflected in work cultures. In so doing they are transforming their lives, the workplace and the larger society.

THE POWER OF SPIRIT

People are much more than a bundle of skills and knowledge, as many managers think. People also come to work armed with a spirit, a life-giving principle, that is concerned also with higher moral qualities. In a work context, spirituality is perceived to include a much broader range of experience, while religion and faith are seen as limiting the discussion to experiences that arise in traditional religious institutions or ways of thinking (Vaill, 1989). Defined this way, people—workers—engage in work with their whole soul, whether or not management theory or some managers—or management pundits—take note of it.

People want more from work than just excitement, a good job and a chance to be promoted. The modern work force is more intelligent and informed than that of a previous generation, and most important, it is more demanding. Today's workers come to work wanting to take responsibility, accept challenging work and make a contribution to corporate success from the foundation of their whole self, not to use a few skills, knowledge and abilities that are delineated in a sterile position description. They want meaningful work; they want to make a legitimate contribution to the betterment of themselves, others and their community.

Success in today's global market demands innovation, creativity, commitment and vision from all of us. We cannot easily reduce these capacities to writing in a position description, nor can they be measured on standard measures. Yet they are essential for the kind of employee every leader or manager wants and our textbooks advocate: people who work hard, are innovative, exciting, curious, highly ethical, constantly learning, a joy to be with and seek both growth and financial rewards. Of course church and corporate life differ. Of course leaders should build into any corporate culture a distinction between corporate rights and personal rights to the private enjoyment of religious convictions. But there should also be mechanisms to allow workers to see the larger societal purposes and results of their work. There should be an opportunity to make personal, individual contributions in response to their highest-order spiritual goals in addition to the routine of day-to-day work. Spiritually-tuned workers want to do something great and feel guilty if they fall short.

18

Understanding Spiritual
Leadership at Work

Accepting people's inner sense of spirituality in work settings identifies and clarifies our core values, ethics and beliefs and places them in context. Our inner standards of right conduct come out of our spirituality, not policy, and are crucial to work success. These inner standards are the motivating force for all life and are the guide for life's actions. It is the underlying element in all major business decisions: hiring, firing, deciding with whom to do business, whom to trust, where to work and how much of our life-force to invest in that work. It helps us think more clearly and deeply.

THE FORCE OF SPIRIT

Our inner sense of the spiritual gives us a value system beyond the boss or the corporation and their policies and procedures. The Christian Bible and all other spiritual value systems suggest a similar prioritized ranking of an inner moral standard above materialistic rewards. The spiritual standard of moral conduct we adopt as our guide cannot help but shape our behaviors on the job, whether or not it is formally included in theory and practice. It increases and focuses caring behaviors. It changes the character of internal communications systems. It is the source of our most powerful and personal values. It increases effective team membership. It creates a dynamic, appealing and creative culture.

A sense of our spiritual self has always been a part of the dynamic of leader-follower relationships. That it is only now receiving popular—and some academic and practitioner—attention does not take anything away from its pervasive power and utility as an important tool in the leader's tool kit. Our spiritual capacities are a significant, even vital, part of our true self and a powerful force in shaping our actions at work and elsewhere. And it has always been so.

The current discussion of spirituality as an issue for serious debate by business leaders is not propelled by their concerns about personal faith or religious traditions (Terry, 1994). Rather, it arises out of the feelings of disconnection many workers feel. Spirituality provides the basis for a new connection between workers and the leaders who want to guide their professional lives. Spirituality in the workplace is moving workers and leaders away from ideas of us against them, and even from the idea of taking ownership, toward ideas of a unifying stewardship (McMillen, 1994).

AN OLD/NEW DEFINITION OF SUCCESS

Spirituality is a new tool leaders can use to respond to this worker disconnection by making a concern for spiritual needs a part of their vision for the team. A focus on spiritual needs lets leaders and led unite on a common ground—at the metaphysical, not the transactional, level. As we make this connection, fleeting differences of policy or procedure lose essential meaning. Workers and leaders can accept these differences in the assurance that they share common core values and purposes.

Life is a challenge to overcome external pressures to conform and be authentic to the inner voice challenging us to personal excellence. Many people struggle to respond directly to their inner voice in contrast with the demands placed on them for external compromise. Because we spend so much time at work, the workplace has become the site where much of this struggle takes place. Workers are coming to recognize that many of the failings of our society are due to our past disregard for core values and a willingness to let the elites of the world lead us astray.

Spirituality in the workplace enhances personal liberty. Of course, for many of us, if we don't take money, we can't survive, and then, of course, we can't do anything. But people want to associate with the corporate team for something more than just bottom-line economic rewards. They need to be free to innovate, to alter their work processes, to do the organization's work in different ways, or even to do other work because in so doing they see personal spiritual growth and development. Spiritual values are the glue holding leader and led together. Leaders who cannot or will not see the power of spirit in what they do, who they think they are and who their followers are and want to become, will fail to attract tomorrow's workers.

Spirituality enlarges our soul and gives it purpose. In business it means the corporation really lives by values such as living with integrity, treating every person with dignity, finding joy in what we do for a living and experiencing the exhilaration of true collaboration. Covey (1992) says people are determinedly seeking spiritual and moral anchors in their lives and their work. They are feeling the need for values that don't change.

Spiritual leaders see spirit as the basis for everything. They cannot imagine looking at the world in any other way (Magaziner, 1994). They are people who feel safe outside what they know and who are passionate about what they have never tried. Spirituality is the process of living out a set of deeply held personal values, of honoring forces greater than the self. Recognition of the spirit of work and of workers endows the corporation with soul—or at least recognizes the soul of the corporation that we have previously ignored.

Society is increasingly viewing corporations as adaptable organizations, made up of many self-reliant, independent small organizations. This idea runs counter to scientific materialism, a philosophy dominant in the earlier part of this century. It is a global change in mind-set, a shift of an entire society's reality from the scientific to the spiritual (Harman, 1992). It is a shifting of our core work environment.

PRACTICAL (WORK) SPIRITUALITY

Spirit expresses itself in beauty, aesthetics and in our relationships with our customers, our employees and ourselves (Jacobs, 1994). Spirituality is an integration or balancing of people, teams and the social system. At the personal level, it means sacrificing part of our own deepest being so that devoting ourselves to our work experiences is not loss but fulfillment of self. From a system perspective it is shaping our cultural institutions and then letting them shape us.

Corporate leaders succeed who model their leadership on a comprehensive picture of humankind that respects all the dimensions of our being and subordinates our material and instinctive dimensions to our interior spiritual ones. It is a union of spirit and work through a reaffirmation of the moral point of view in business decision making. It is balancing the pursuit of purpose in the face of tendencies to overemphasize overarching goals and undervalue moral responsibility when it interferes with the achievement of goals.

Of course, there is some skepticism about the new emphasis on spirituality in the workplace. Most will not doubt the accuracy of the observation, but they do question its desirability. Some see it as a dangerous intrusion on worker privacy: an invitation to inefficiency and unaccountability. Unquestionably, it challenges a safe secularity in the quest for ethical values. Nevertheless, the key questions for today's managers and leaders are no longer issues of task and structure but questions of spirit (Hawley, 1993).

Our soul is integrated with all parts of our life. We respond to the force of moral and ethical values gained throughout our whole life as much, and perhaps more, than we guide our actions solely in terms of organization-set standards. Seen this way spirituality is an essential foundation for the quality of the decisions we make. It moderates and contains the day-to-day life challenges that often cause us to question "right or wrong" choices. It subliminally shapes the opinions that we see as viable.

We integrate our spirituality into the secular team through all our behavior. Spirituality has to have an effect on all behavior and choice, including work behavior. As people understand the difference between religion and spirituality, spirituality can take its place in leadership theory-building as an important part of all individual and group action. We draw on our core values in dealing with people every day. Our spirituality helps us to think and act according to these values.

Our beliefs and moral visions determine our career paths and all that we do along these paths. Present business practices that dehumanize the workplace, treat workers as economic objects and value corporate profit above humanness run counter to the intuitive forces within all of us. Spirituality goes beyond ideas of vision and mission and provides the necessary underpinning to make them work in our personal and professional lives. Operationally, spirituality implies a relationship with something beyond the self. It is a means of personal and group integration.

It is in this latter context that spirituality has a place in our work lives. We can define spiritual leaders as those who respond to the real significance of someone or something (Fairholm, 1997). They are people who live by a higher moral standard of conduct in their relationships. This inner moral standard affects all we do and become at work levels as well as at social levels of existence.

This kind of spiritual leadership is in demand today. Successful corporate operations are those that respect individual rights and dignity. Often without explicitly recognizing it, spirituality is at the heart of much of the popular literature on values-based transformational leadership. Transforming leadership based on core values counters the secular tendency toward fragmentation of our spirit (Senge, 1990) that is the common description of present (and past) work cultures. Far too many people live their corporate lives separate from other people, from nature, from the environment, from everything.

We can connect spirituality at work to ideas about employee ownership, attitudes of cooperation and honoring diversity, while also confirming a sense of corporate community. Spirit makes use of the idea of creative work, work with a deeper sense of life-purpose. It defines work that lets people feel they are making a difference, creating meaning, being fully alive, living with integrity, developing sacredness in their relationships. It involves turning the corporation into a learning community where everyone can grow.

Spiritual leadership asks us to reject past models of human leadership that focused on values of self-interest. Earlier models implicitly focused on the values of power, wealth and prestige. In contrast, the transcendent values of spiritual leaders include a rejection of self-interest and a focus on servanthood. They focus on core ethical values, including integrity, independence, freedom, justice, family and caring.

These corporate values draw heavily on principles from Judeo-Christian teachings (Erteszek, 1983). They reflect core American values (Fairholm, 1991). They reinforce our traditional beliefs in the dignity of all people. They define corporate leaders as the trustees, or stewards, of life and resources. They reflect ideas of what is good for individuals and for groups. They are convictions about what will promote the faith or protect the country or build companies or transform our schools. Spiritual leaders link our interior world of moral reflection and the outer world of work and social relationships.

SPIRITUAL LEADERSHIP AT WORK

There is little to guide us in applying spiritual leadership in the more or less prescribed confines of process and procedures peculiar to corporate life. Nevertheless, we are also responsive to the force of our spiritual standards at work. The work we do, the people we interact with and the kind of skills we use all challenge or reinforce our sense of self. They have a spiritual dimension.

Work can be a drain on our spiritual capacity, or it can be a source of renewal and growth. Work defines in large part who we are socially and, perhaps, helps shape who we are at our core self. When that work is sensitive to our spiritual needs, we grow and mature, and so do those around us. When it ignores or is antagonistic to our spiritual sensibilities, we encounter stress, which is sometimes so severe as to cause physical or emotional trauma.

Leaders who accept the challenge to relate to followers in terms of a shared reverence for spiritual things can add another tool to their professional stock. Their spirituality helps leaders understand themselves and others better. It helps the leader motivate and inspire others. Spirituality is another source of strength for the leader. Spirit-centered interaction helps leaders and led work more fully together.

The spirit-leader model integrates a variety of implicit work ideas recently made explicit by a few people. These ideas include issues of optimism, balance, capacity and continuous improvement. Spiritual leadership is also an amalgam of culture, mood, moral tone and awareness of the inner core self. It sets the standard of excellence for the group.

Leaders are moral architects; they liberate the best in others. Spiritual leaders expand work-life concerns to include "soft" ideas of meaning, fidelity and caring. Leaders communicate their inner strength to others. They create bonds that fulfill people's needs. They help followers find the sacred everywhere. As work-resources trustees, leaders help unite the group and focus collective attention on mutually desired results. They are stewards of virtues. They create oneness in the group.

The key elements of spiritual leadership have a dynamic relationship to each other and manifest themselves in leader-follower interactivity. Spiritual leadership is a dynamic process of building special skills such as visioning, servanthood and work-task competence. Spiritual leaders engage in special processes of building community, encouraging personal wholeness, engaging in stewardship and creating a higher moral standard. They seek one primary goal among all the others challenging the leader's time and attention: continuous improvement of the individual and the group.

A working definition of spiritual leadership today must include ideas like teaching our followers correct principles and the application of techniques that enable self-governance. It is creating cultures where followers can function freely with the leader and within the work group, subject to only broad accountability. It is redefining the leader's role in terms of servant and steward. It asks leaders to provide environments that both recognize and feed the spirit in all coworkers.

Acting out of our spiritual self is hard. It asks leaders to use new untapped energies. Leaders gather strength from their inner conviction that their vision values are correct, right for their followers, true for them and the group. Added strength comes from the support of their followers as they come to share the leader's vision values, accept the constraints defined by those values and actively participate in accomplishing the joint vision (Fairholm, 1997).

We can list a variety of communities of support leaders can draw on. The other people we interact with are a spiritually renewing source. Some are renewed spiritually by the activities in which they engage.

Still other sources include community and social groups. These sources of personal spiritual renewal are useful because they confirm and revitalize our values, ethics and beliefs. They provide a source for restoring own spiritual self.

INTEGRATION OF SPIRITUALITY INTO SECULAR WORK GROUPS

There are, of course, obvious risks in trying to act authentically in terms of values formerly relegated to religion. Few will argue that the typical workplace resembles the average church or that typical workers are like the average believer. But religious believers are on the job eight or ten hours a day, and they want to relate the best of themselves to the activity in which they spend the bulk of their time. The integration process may be helped as leaders try to understand self and others better. It is facilitated as the leader trusts others, because trust motivates others. Spirituality is another source of strength for leaders. It helps them know their coworkers better.

Some elements of a model for applying spiritual concepts on the job are becoming visible. One element is process thinking. Process thinking is thinking of the corporation as a circular process of complex interactivity. It provides a new perspective from which to view organizations and their leaders. Another is self-esteem. When seen from the perspective of the inner soul, motivation takes on a different character. It becomes a task to inspire and encourage others to be their best selves through innovation, intuition, spontaneity, compassion, openness, receptivity to new ideas, honesty, caring, dignity and respect for people.

Covey's (1991) leadership standard helps resolve several dilemmas encountered in applying spiritual leadership. His principle-centered leadership focuses on the whole person of the leader. It is an approach that calls into play the soul of the leader in defining himself or herself to the team.

Leading others today asks us to employ the whole person (Hawley, 1993). Leaders need to use their head, the linear thinking part. They must also engage their heart, the feeling side, along with their body, with its physical muscle, health and wellness aspects. They need to make use of their spirit, the deep inner self, which is striving for inner peace, happiness, contentment, meaning and purpose. Both the spiritual and the worldly coexist as a unified overlapping whole. They are two parts of the same force that activates work life.

Moving toward our higher spiritual self creates spiritual energy, the power that spirit activates. There is power in good thoughts. Leadership arouses and channels this human energy. Belief is a force that shapes all human affairs. Belief is power thinking. It is focusing thoughts to produce actions. Belief is something we are as much as it is something we believe. It is the basis for doing anything, not the actual doing.

19

Application of Spiritual Leadership at Work

The leadership famine in our social, business and civic communities stems in part from the fact that many would-be leaders focus on special groups and not the larger encompassing community. The leadership gap also has been deepened because too few would-be leaders have been willing to give up tight control of their group members to become the orchestrators of their followers' independent actions.

Rather than exercise control, the ideal leader for today's business climate continually seek to bring out the best in people. They are sensitive to others' needs to grow, change and mature. They vary their responses according to the person and the situation. These leaders believe that their real success is in the successes of the people they lead. The new breed of spiritual leader understands that when people feel cared about, they will go to extremes to help those who help them.

The nature of leadership stems from the leader's personality and soul rather than from just his or her behavior (Keifer, 1992). Contemporary models have lost sight of the need to energize, inspire and enthuse workers, not just supervise them. Leaders seek to create a climate in which leader and led bring forward the best they have to offer. True leadership is setting standards and values and persuading others to accept them as personal and group guides. By setting clear standards and helping others grow within these standards in mind-stretching and ability-stretching ways, we will experience an infinite variety in results. For the individual, this can result in closing the gap between what he or she is and what he or she might become.

Leaders do not place themselves at the center; they place others there. When people perceive that their bosses have high credibility, they are significantly more likely to tell others of their affiliation with the organization, feel a strong sense of team spirit and see their personal values as consistent with those of the team.

ELEMENTS OF SPIRITUAL LEADERSHIP

Spiritual leadership involves many ideas, some common in the values-based transformational leadership model, some more commonly seen in metaphysical, religious or philosophical literature. Leadership deals with a range of elements. Following Fairholm (1997), we can organize these elements of spiritual leadership into the pattern shown below in Figure 2.

Figure 2
Elements of Spiritual Leadership

Category	Elements
Community	Ceremony, Culture, Oneness, Wholeness
Continuous Improvement	Capacity, Corporate Health
Competence	Balance, Credibility, Trust, Power
A Higher Moral Standard	Positive Affirmation, Ethics, Heart, Integrity, Love, Presence, Meaning, Morals
Servanthood	Liberation
Spirituality	Corporate Spirit, Emotions, Truth, Sacred, Non-sectarian Spirit, Relationships
Stewardship	Team, Trustee
Visioning	Values, State of Mind

THE SPIRITUAL LEADERSHIP MODEL

We can abstract a skeleton outline of the spiritual-leadership virtual environment from these elements. This outline addresses what is essentially a new environment, a new culture of leadership, one that demands new, untried solutions. This model tries to embody those values, traits and practices proven effective in various kinds of organizations and with some individual leaders over time.

This pattern recognizes the whole person for the first time in modern

Figure 3
Model of the Spiritual Leadership Model

Spiritual Leadership Tasks	Spiritual Leadership Process Technologies	The Prime Leadership Goal

leadership. It accepts that people come to work owning all of their human qualities, not just the skills, knowledge and abilities needed at a given time by the employing corporation. Workers today—and perhaps, always—come to work armed with, and ready to use, their total life experiences. They have and want to use all of their skills (McGregor, 1960).

Leaders cannot conduct spiritual leadership or any other kind of leadership in a vacuum. It is a dynamic process engaging in unique ways the model elements. Figure 3 pictures the dynamics and inter-relationship patterns of this new leadership approach.

The brief descriptions and elaboration of the eight core ideas of spiritual leadership summarized below helps us encompass this version of leadership for the twenty-first century.

Spiritual Leadership Tasks

The three spiritual leadership tasks are task competence, vision setting and servanthood.

Task Competence

Competency in four kinds of tasks: (1) teaching, (2) trusting (3) inspiring and (4) acquiring knowledge about the actual work, the tasks, of the group is essential in leadership. Development and use of these spiritual leadership technologies are critical parts of spirit-based leadership. Spiritual leaders who have high self-confidence and a conviction of their moral rightness transfer these qualities to followers (Burns, 1978; Maccoby, 1976; Fairholm, 1991, 1994b).

Vision Setting

Leadership is about creating and then sharing meaning and intentions. The source of the leader's vision is his or her individual sense of spirituality. Visions deal with contentment, capacity, equanimity, detachment and connectedness. Spiritual leaders develop vision statements that foster the development of cooperation, mutual caring and dedication to work.

Servanthood

Leaders lead because they choose to serve others. They serve by making available to followers information, time, attention, material and other resources and the higher corporate purposes that give meaning to the work. The leadership of service asks leaders to create and facilitate a culture of self-leadership.

Four Spiritual Leadership Processes

The spiritual leadership process includes building community within the group and a sense of personal spiritual wholeness in both leader and led. Spiritual leaders set, and live by, a higher moral standard and ask others to share that standard. They act in a stewardship role, forming a shared responsibility team (Bradford and Cohen, 1984).

Building Community

Spirit-based leadership denotes the creation of harmony from often diverse, sometimes opposing, organizational, human, system and program factions. It is an exercise of community building, of making one out of many. It is a task of generalizing deeply held values, beliefs and principles of action in ways that all stakeholders will find acceptable and energizing. Spiritual leadership recognizes the simultaneous need we all have to be free to act in terms of our own reality *and* to be part of a similarly focused group.

Wholeness

Spiritual leaders are concerned with the whole person, not just the specific skills they have that are useful to the current work being done. Relationships with followers, therefore, consider what the individual can now do, what they want to do and what their capacity is to prepare for this more inclusive work.

Setting a Higher Moral Standard

Spiritual leaders set the moral tone for the group. They set the individual and corporate mood. Leadership is about sharing intentions that raise the levels of human conduct. Leaders take pains to understand—and see that stakeholders also understand—the natural and logical consequences that flow from their actions.

Stewardship

Leaders understand that their leadership is held in trust for a temporary period. They may propose plans, choices and programs, but followers have an opportunity to consent before the actions taken are universally accepted. They set the values foundation for the group and model these values in their actions. Only when the core values serve the best interests of team members is stewardship possible or spiritual leadership present.

The Single Goal of Leadership: Continuous Improvement

Leaders seek to liberate the best in people. The movement toward increased quality throughout the corporation is a cultural challenge more than a technological one. This task is one of education of the heart more than training of the head or hand. It is a task of leadership and not merely managerial resource control. It is a values-change task. It sets up different, challenging expectations for all workers.

20

Applying Spiritual Leadership

Nourishing the spirit at work asks leaders to consider and respond to yet another dimension of human life beyond those traditionally identified with leader-follower relationships. Application of spiritual leadership therefore means creating circumstances where followers can function freely with the leader and within their work, subject to only broad accountability. It means redefining the leader in servant and steward terms.

There is peculiar power in this new leadership technology, which encompasses a holistic conception of the corporation both as an economic enterprise *and* as a human system. This holistic approach addresses the personal as well as the professional lives of workers (Kouzes and Posner, 1993). The challenge is to achieve and maintain a renewing balance between work and family and between the personal and professional areas of life.

Three specific spirit-leader technologies complete this evolving spiritual leadership model. Individually, they represent foundation stones upon which leaders can build their unique leadership ethic. These foundation stones are morality, stewardship and community. All of the other techniques and approaches used by spiritual leaders are subsumed within these three fundamental technologies.

SETTING A HIGHER MORAL STANDARD

The work we do has a moral dimension. Most individuals want to do good work and to contribute to the success of the team. Unfortunately, in too many work situations we have been led to believe that there is one standard for private morality and another for business morality and conduct (Nair, 1994). Not so! Morality argues for one standard, which is applicable in personal, social, economic and all other aspects of life.

We cannot compromise some ideals. We must defend them. Spiritual leaders prefer to compete with some opposing ideas, rather than accommodate them. They are sometimes outspoken and deliberately confrontational when they assess alternative value systems. They affirm the superior value of the spiritual over other leadership models. While traditional functions and roles may be similar, spiritual leaders apply them in overtly moral ways.

Including a moral dimension in our choices and actions helps us think and act beyond narrowly defined business and political interests. Such leadership will give meaning and purpose to our working lives. Arguably, this is the only way we can attract tomorrow's workers to our vision and our goals.

We can define ethical leadership as both a process that asks questions about what is right and wrong and a mode of conduct that sets an example for others about the rightness or wrongness of particular actions (Kouzes and Posner, 1992). The infrastructure of spiritual leadership is based on an idea of moral service. The soul of ethics and of spiritual leadership is love. Spiritual leadership rejects coercion to secure desired goals. It is non-interference with human freedom and choices, though these choices may entail some painful decisions and shifts in priorities. Elements of moral spiritual leadership include

Building Shared Values

Spiritual leaders inspire a sense of shared community values. Common values provide the basis for the sanctions systems (punishment and reward systems) that define the morality of community members and determine the group's measures of success.

Integrity

Integrity is a function of feeling whole, total, connected. Moral integrity involves a willingness to say what needs to be said and not needlessly say what may hurt another. It demands self-discipline, strengthening the self in terms of inner prompting.

Vision Setting

Spiritual leaders exhibit a sustained ability to build consensus and lead democratically in terms of a shared vision.

Sharing Meaning

Spiritual leaders create meaning for others. They engage the heart (Kouzes and Posner, 1987). This leadership task includes formal relationships, of course; but more importantly, the leader creates an ethical base that provides the context for shared values, meaning and focus to the team structure. Leaders (not managers) focus the power present in work relationships. Leaders shape the cultural surround within which the corporation and its people operate. They provide ethical direction, incentive, inspiration and support to individuals and teams.

Enabling

Moral leaders train, educate and coach followers in appropriate team ethics. They provide motivation, involve followers in appropriate networks and then free them from situational constraints that may hamper their growth toward full moral effectiveness.

Influence and Power

The measure of leadership is not structural, but attitudinal (DePree, 1989). Until followers choose to accept the leader's power, the leader cannot lead. The leader's words and actions combine to inspire all stakeholders to desired levels of performance by making full use of individual abilities, interests and capacities. It is, thus, a power tool for leaders.

Intuition

Intuition is knowledge gained without rational thought (Rowan, 1986). Spiritual leadership, moral leadership, any kind of leadership must tap intuitive values held in common by the group. Intuition taps ingrained ideas and values, values that are also held by group members that give spiritual leaders their moral legitimacy.

Risk Taking

Spiritual leaders need to challenge existing work and team processes (Kouzes and Posner, 1987). They do not simply accept current work codes or existing structural relationships. Rather, spiritual leaders are pioneers. They try to produce real change that meets people's enduring needs regardless of the risk.

Service

The spiritual leader is a servant committed to the principles of spiritual relationships defined above. The leader's job is to prepare followers to provide high-quality, excellent service to clients, customers and citizens. Rather than attempt to dominate followers, spiritual leaders *go to work for them*—providing all things necessary for follower success.

Transformation

Spiritual leaders transform themselves, others and the organization. In the process, they help create a new scale of meaning within which followers can see their lives in terms of the larger community. The spiritual leader's role is to change the lives of followers and of institutions in ways that enhance both. Spiritual leaders convert followers into leaders.

Common Ethical Values

Common values shared by group members provide the basis of the strategy that defines team morality and determines its ethical sanctions system. Our spiritual values are always with us whether or not we are aware of them. They are the activating mechanisms of our moral character. They are part of our self-analysis as we observe and reflect on our actions and judgements of events. Moral values are part of all aspects of life.

Being moral is a matter of personal and professional character. Character is a cluster of related attributes that includes morality, ethics, honesty and humane values. It is knowing that the actions we take are right: that is, acceptable to the group and ourselves. Spiritual leaders understand that all people have the inalienable right of free moral choice. They know that the irrevocable law of the harvest—return good for good, evil for evil—operates in our lives.

Primarily, leaders who take charge, set the moral climate and are accountable for their actions and results manage the business of being ethically moral. Operationally, morality involves following ethical standards and patiently sticking to one's purpose. It is feeling good about one self and reflecting on the ideals of current business questions but also thinking about our actions in terms of our inner standards of right and wrong.

STEWARDSHIP

As we bring spirituality to the workplace, a new idea of the individual in the group emerges, an idea called classically (and revived recently) stewardship. The values-based transformational leadership idea of ownership shifts to stewardship (McMillen, 1994) in spiritual leadership. Ownership connotes possession and control. Stewardship connotes holding work resources in trust for a temporary period. In a stewardship team, power is inherent in each steward to help accomplish the stewardship team's—not just the steward's own—ends. It is by sharing equally all power that we become one, united.

We base stewardship on self-directed free moral choice. Every steward has the same rights and is subject to identical limitations in the exercise of self-direction. This sharing of power preserves harmony and good will. The leader is also a steward and subject to the same limitations and advantages of other stewards. Leaders ensure every steward has a single voice in sitting in council with other stewards and a single vote in the power of consent. Stewardships preserve oneness by procedures that enhance common consent. In this way each steward is protected against unjust or dominating leaders.

Spiritual leadership is operating in service to, rather than in control of, those around us. It is less prescriptive. It has more to do with being accountable than it does with being responsible for what the group creates or with defining, prescribing and telling others what to do. Stewardship is not a single guiding principle but part of a triumvirate that includes empowerment and partnership as well as stewardship. The principle of stewardship brings accountability, while partnership balances responsibility. It is a sharing of a governance system where each member holds control and responsibility in trust for the group as a team. It is a relationship system based on mutual accountability.

A steward role asks leader and led to risk losing class distinctions and privilege in the pursuit of living out a set of values and creating a team where members personally reclaim the institution as their own. Stewardship operates at the whole-person—spiritual—level of existence and interrelationship. It includes ideas of team work and individual free choice.

The Stewardship Team

The team—stewardship unit—is critical in stewardship ideas. As members come to identify with the stewardship team, they are participating at a level beyond consensus and compromise. At this level, a member does not merely accept another member's position. Instead, it becomes a course of action all members accept, support and foster. Spiritual leaders base relationships on shared values, habits and practices that assure respect for others' rights. Stewardship is integral to ideas of corporate community. Membership in a stewardship team asks spiritual leaders to lead the stewardship team but also play a role as a member of the team community.

Personal liberty—the capacity to make free-will choices—is integral to the idea of stewardship. The expectation that we can be free to make our own choices in our groups is fully American. Many of the most important choices we make—that make life happy or sad—are not individual choices, but group choices. A stewardship community lets members make choices about whom to partner with, what products or services to buy from internal or external suppliers, how to spend discretionary funds and time and how to serve their customers.

The idea of adding a stewardship orientation to corporate governance is new. Many leaders have no operational experience with this concept and, therefore, cannot immediately visualize either their steward-leader role in the corporation or their part in building stewardship teams. While the idea may be appealing, many don't know how stewardship works in practice. The following example may help operationalize what is, for many, just a good idea.

Stewardship is an expectation of production in proportion to what is given. It involves accounting. It involves no interference with the steward until the time of accounting. The stewardship team is based on decentralization. How we do it is as important as what we do. Stewardship teams eliminate class distinctions. All team members—stewards—are equal. All have an equal opportunity for managing their stewardship. All have equal access to available rewards. They are equal in social status. The steward-leader is also a steward and subject to the same limitations and advantages of other stewards. Every steward has a single voice in stewardship councils and a single vote.

Stewards' contributions to the team are not measured in terms of differential recognition. Status and hierarchical distinctions are absent (Deming, 1986). No one member is more important to the team than any other. Loss of the contribution of anyone diminishes the team and jeopardizes its success since the team is not whole without all its members.

The Stewardship Team Structure

The basic entities of the stewardship team are the individual steward, the stewardship leader and the team membership, who form a council of the team and a higher-level council. All stewards are coequals with all others in the stewardship team. Each steward has the right to exercise power in forming the particulars of his or her stewardship within the team.

A process of accountability takes place between coequal people who share the desire to be initiators of work systems. The center of initiation and decision resides with all stewards. However, the steward-leader retains the power of counsel and consent. Appeals from the leader's decisions go to the stewardship team council or to the higher-level coun-

Figure 4
Typical Stewardship Team Structure

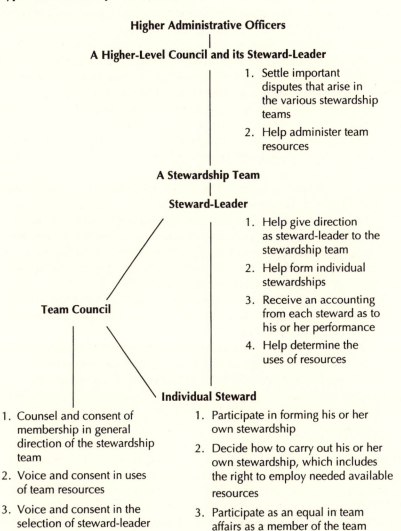

Higher Administrative Officers

A Higher-Level Council and its Steward-Leader

1. Settle important disputes that arise in the various stewardship teams
2. Help administer team resources

A Stewardship Team

Steward-Leader

1. Help give direction as steward-leader to the stewardship team
2. Help form individual stewardships
3. Receive an accounting from each steward as to his or her performance
4. Help determine the uses of resources

Team Council

Individual Steward

1. Counsel and consent of membership in general direction of the stewardship team
2. Voice and consent in uses of team resources
3. Voice and consent in the selection of steward-leader

1. Participate in forming his or her own stewardship
2. Decide how to carry out his or her own stewardship, which includes the right to employ needed available resources
3. Participate as an equal in team affairs as a member of the team council

cil. The steward decides how to carry out his or her stewardship. Each steward has equal voice with other stewards in the running of the stewardship team.

The steward-leader's role is that of servant rather than master. By assisting stewards to achieve their potential, steward-leaders multiply the contribution they otherwise could make. Their role as servant encourages responses from those they serve. They foster cooperation, not competition. The steward-leader is required to obtain the acquiescence of the stewardship team before giving direction. By doing this, the steward-leader gains the use of the best experience, and the maximum creative energy and wisdom, in the stewardship team.

Since each steward determines his or her own resource needs, the steward-leader is relieved from the troublesome task of allocating resources. He or she is relieved from the many personnel problems stemming from greed, jealousy and rivalry. Leaders give only general direction to the stewardship team with respect to administrative matters. They help determine the nature of each steward's stewardship. They receive the steward's accounting and judge whether he or she has been discerning and steadfast. They share the power of determining the uses of the resources of the stewardship team.

The team as a council allocates the resources of the team. Decisions are based on the principle of common agreement. Assuming the resource allocator is faithful and wise, he or she settles important disputes between the stewards and the steward-leader. Each stewardship team member is equal in all things. The goals of the stewardship team council and the team itself are to develop each member to the fullest, while attaining the desired team work outcomes.

A higher-level council settles important disputes that arise in the various stewardship teams. They also help administer team resources, especially when shortages occur.

Figure 4 is a diagram of a typical stewardship team that can be developed showing formal relationships among the four actors in the stewardship leadership model. Both relationships and essential responsibilities are shown.

BUILDING COMMUNITY

Holistic spiritual leadership is no longer only a choice. It is a need in today's world (Pinchot and Pinchot, 1994). Workplaces are communities in which many of us live much of our productive lives. We need, therefore, to know what we can about how to make productive communities. Bureaucracies cannot do this. They segment responsibilities so that humanity becomes a departmental, rather than a universal, responsibility.

Service to a sense of community plays a critical role in the development of spiritual leadership potential. Spiritual leaders create cooperative, action-oriented communities that, in turn, provide the environment and the culture within which leaders can operate out of a sense of spirituality. The time has come to engage in the production of new corporate designs focusing on interactive communities of enabled moral leaders and followers.

The task for leadership in the coming century is to transform work organizations into viable, attractive communities capable of attracting workers with needed skills and talents. Building attractive workplace communities counters present trends to worker anomie and alienation. A sense of community invigorates members' lives with a sense of purpose and a feeling of belonging to an integrated group that is doing something worthwhile.

Community is from the root word meaning "with unity." Community-oriented corporations operate out of shared visions, beliefs and values. Leaders build a workplace community by providing this common vision. No community—society—can function well unless most members behave most of the time because they voluntarily heed their moral commitments and social responsibilities (Etzioni, 1993). Leaders bring unity to organizations. They strengthen and use corporation culture, and they define new ceremonies and rituals that bring people together to form communities. Leaders transform work teams into communities.

The present resurgence of interest in flexibility, cultural inclusiveness and full acceptance of differences in individual group members is antithetical to community—and to leadership itself (Fairholm, 1994b). While emotionally attractive, it is operationally toxic. Leaders build group relationships, not just membership. They create corporate spirit, a spiritual force that honors high performance, compassion, empathy for others and individual contributions. But it is a focused force that builds wholeness and drives out factions.

This kind of community is a powerful force. It directs the lives of members, both as individuals and as participants in their relationships with others within the organization. The communities to which we belong act as emotional environments that can block acceptance of alternative cultures. Community values can isolate the individual member from other cultural associations. They can also unite individuals into strong coalitions of mutually interdependent teams. The key to attaining this latter result is the strength of community the leader builds.

Building community becomes, therefore, a critical leadership task. We need to focus on communities of equal leaders and followers. We need to engage the people making up these communities in meaningful work, in work that ennobles them and their colleagues and customers. The workplace is a community in which many of us live much of our productive lives. We need, therefore, to know what we can about how to make work communities, not only productive, but personally inspiring.

The corporation is defined by ideas of authority, power, bureaucracy, competition and profit. Adding the idea of community, however, adds factors of consistency, democracy, cooperation, interdependence and mutual benefit. Modern corporate team and social theory and practice have separated us from traditional communities: the family, the farm, the land, the neighborhood. The family and the small social neighborhoods of the past recognized and legitimized spirit.

Contemporary social and work structures have divested modern organizations of a place for our spirit or soul. Free individuals require a community that backs them up against encroachments on their sense of independence by society's formal institutions, including economic ones. The resurgence of the idea of community is a reaction against a controlled social process that robs people of their sense of self and substitutes a senseless conformity to a sterile, abstract and spiritless system. As people come to recognize the power of the corporation to shape not only their own lives but those of their children, they are forcing business to change—to be more accommodating to spiritual values.

Holistic leadership is not an option in today's world (Pinchot and Pinchot, 1994). Many of the most important choices we make—that make life happy or sad—are not individual choices, but group choices. We have come to know (again) that the important, meaningful outcomes in life cannot be attained alone. We need other people to help us become our best selves. Many of us live much of our productive lives in workplace communities (Brown, 1992). We need, therefore, to know what we can about how to make productive communities, for this is the place we make ourselves.

Today most Americans relate more to their work or organizational relationships than they do to any other social grouping, with the possible exception of the family. They value their corporate citizenship sometimes more than they do their citizenship in the state. This fact influences how they act, what they value, how they measure themselves and their actions. Control of environmental stimuli, therefore, becomes the essential mechanism for control over worker performance. Controlling—managing—the corporate culture becomes the central managerial task. This is, at heart, a value-displacement activity.

We cannot buy people's citizenship in the team. It is voluntary. Freedom of action—autonomy—is a value implicit in corporate citizenship. The use of authority must fall within the employee's zone of acceptability, or group members will resist it (Barnard, 1968). We can define corporate citizenship as the acceptance of the corporate values set by the leader and action in concert with these values. The association is either an ethical association or a contractual, economic or social one. In either case we can define the association not by mere membership, but by the acceptance and commitment shown by actions that conform to the firm's values.

Similarly, obligation, consent and participation are also elements of corporate citizenship. Individuals have rights the corporation must honor. They also have a responsibility to the corporation to be involved, committed and supportive. Corporate citizenship is a mutual relationship with opportunities and duties on both sides. Whether the relationship is total or limited to tasks, corporate citizenship asks both leader and follower to accept common values and act according to them. Values become the adhesive of citizenship in the group.

Spiritual community is a basic change in the way one thinks about work and all life. In a community, members have undergone a fundamental shift in orientation from the belief that people must cope with life and are powerless to the conviction that they are individually and collectively empowered to create their future and shape their destiny. Community leaders are custodians of corporate values. These leaders empower and coach others to create what they want. They structure rewards and incentives. These leaders specify personal and corporate values and belief structures. They energize these values through habits, they help create the free flow of information, the physical work flow and management processes.

OTHER SPIRITUAL LEADERSHIP TECHNIQUES

The movement today is from the age of producing to the age of thinking (Marquardt and Reynolds, 1994). Results come more from the heart than from the mind. Tomorrow's organizations will engage the mind and heart (the soul) of all stakeholders (Pinchot and Pinchot, 1994). This movement assumes workers are thinking contributors, not just physical extensions of the manager's capacities, ideas and creativity.

We need radically new organizational structures and systems to meet these challenges of a more complex and turbulent business world (Mitroff, 1994). The challenge is to build cohesive teams, which include workers and supervisors. It is to create and effectively communicate a strategic vision, institute strong intra-company support systems and create a participative structure that recognizes workers' innate needs and desires as well as company needs.

Leaders will need to become specialists in a variety of new leadership technologies. We review these general spiritual leader technologies briefly below. They constitute foundation features of team and leader orientation upon which spiritual leadership can be practiced.

Developing a healthy organization. Healthy companies radiate a certain vitality and spirit—a deeply held feeling of shared values (Rosen, 1992) that anchors the community. The first duty of spiritual leadership is to insure that the corporate community is healthy. Healthy organizations have several, perhaps obvious, characteristics. They are committed to self-knowledge and development and embody a corporate culture that includes a firm belief in individual decency and manifests a basic respect for individual differences.

Creating a sense of spirituality and moral rightness. We cannot solve our problems with the same mode of thinking that we used to create them. Yet, people are still trying to change the wrong things. We must change context, not just content. Content deals with the surface issues that we can see, hear, touch and smell. Context, on the other hand, concerns the things we cannot touch; it is about the things we feel. Context shifts in the corporation will not occur unless those who are influential in the system go through their own personal transformation and raise their own consciousness. The real goal of an enterprise is the mental and spiritual enrichment of those who take part in it (Nirenberg, 1994).

Fostering the intelligent organization. Choice is a part of all corporate life. Independent decision making and a work environment that supports the freedom to choose will characterize tomorrow's intelligent organization. Tomorrow's intelligent organizations will be communities that develop their people within the freedom of responsible communities.

Global facilitation. Leadership is necessary globally, in the geographic sense and in terms of the whole-person team member. Leading in a global culture asks leaders to connect with others whose support may be vital to their individual, as well as to the group's, success.

Enabling workers. Empowerment is *enabling* followers to be and to do their best. To enable followers we do not have to give away our leadership power. Rather it involves adding to the capability of the team by developing our followers' capacities for action.

Creating esprit de corps. Building esprit involves seeing each follower, customer or client as an original. This kind of esprit leadership requires the leader to adopt a mind-set that values people.

Setting vision. Leaders create the future for the firm through a corporate vision. They articulate a clear, attractive, compelling prediction of what life, the firm and the individuals involved can and should be like. Spiritual leaders continually communicate that vision, focusing the attention and energies of members on attaining this desirable future state of being.

Celebrating successes. Building corporate spirit involves leaders in activities whose primary object is to recognize and honor the individual performance of stakeholders. Celebrations help create and maintain a bond between workers and leaders.

Putting spiritual values to work. Spiritual leadership is a matter of values and ethics. Ethics cannot be measured only by productivity, profitability or sales. Being ethical means creating a climate of ethical expectation.

Bibliography

Adair, John. "Leadership." *International Management* (Europe Edition) 40, no. 4 (April 1985).
———. *Effective Teambuilding*. Brookfield, VT: Gower Publishing Co., 1986.
Adler, M. *Great Ideas from the Great Books*. New York: Washington Square Press, 1969.
Aguayo, Rafael. *Dr. Deming: The American Who Taught the Japanese about Quality*. New York: Carol Publishing Co., 1990.
Autry, James A. *Love and Profit: The Art of Caring Leadership*. New York: Avon Books, 1992.
Badaracco, Joseph L., and Richard R. Ellsworth. "Leadership, Integrity and Conflict." *Management Decision* 30, no. 6 (1992): 29–34.
Barber, Bernard. *The Logic and Limits of Trust*. New Brunswick, NJ: Rutgers University Press, 1983.
Barbour, George P., Thomas W. Fletcher and George A. Sipel. *Excellence in Local Government Handbook*. Washington, DC: International City Management Association, 1984.
Barbour, G. P., and G. A. Sipel. "Excellence in Leadership: Public Sector Model." *Public Management* (August, 1986).
Barker, Joel A. *Future Edge: Discovering the New Rules of Success*. New York: Morrow, 1992.
Barnard, Chester. *Functions of the Executive*. Cambridge, MA: Harvard University Press, 1968.
Barnes, Louis B. "Managing the Paradox of Organizational Trust." *Harvard Business Review* (March–April 1981).
Bass, B. M. *Stogdill's Handbook of Leadership*. New York: The Free Press, 1981.

Bass, B. M., O. A. Waldman and B. Avolio, Jr. "Transformational Leadership and the Falling Domino Effect." *Group and Organizational Studies* 12, no. 1 (1987): 73–87.

Bennis, Warren G., and Burt Nanus. *Leaders: The Strategies for Taking Charge*. New York: Harper & Row, 1985.

Berkley, George. *The Craft of Public Administration*. Newton, MA: Allyn and Bacon Inc., 1984.

Bird, C. *Social Psychology*. New York: Appleton-Century, 1940.

Blake, Robert R., and Jane S. Mouton. *The Managerial Grid*. Houston: Gulf Publishing, 1964.

Block, Peter. *Stewardship: Choosing Service over Self-Interest*. San Francisco: Berrett-Koehler, 1993.

Boyce, W. D. "The Ecology of the Soul." *National Forum, The Phi Kappa Phi Journal* (Winter 1995).

Bradford, David L., and Allen R. Cohen. *Managing for Excellence: The Guide to Developing High Performance in Contemporary Organizations*. New York: John Wiley and Son, 1984.

Brassier, A. "Strategic Vision: A Practical Tool." *The Bureaucrat* (Fall 1985): 23–26.

Brown, Juanita. "Developing a Corporate Community." In John Renesch, ed., *New Traditions in Business: Spirit and Leadership in the 21st Century*. San Francisco: Berrett-Koehler, 1992.

Burns, James M. *Leadership*. New York: Harper and Row, 1978.

Colvin, Robert E. *Transformational Executive Leadership: A Comparison of Culture-Focused and Individual-Focused Leadership Modalities*. Ph.D. diss., Virginia Commonwealth University, 1996.

Conger, Jay A., and Rabindra N. Kanungo. *Charismatic Leadership: The Elusive Factor in Organizational Effectiveness*. San Francisco: Jossey-Bass, 1988.

Cound, Dana M. "A Call for Leadership." *Quality Progress* (March 1987): 11–14.

Covey, Stephen R. *Principle-Centered Leadership*. New York: Summit Books, 1991.

———. "10 Dilemmas." *Executive Excellence* (January 1992): 11–13.

Crane, E. G., B. Lantz and J. Shafritz. *State Government Productivity*. New York: Praeger, 1976.

Crosby, Philip B. *Quality Without Tears: The Art of Hassle-Free Management*. New York: McGraw-Hill, 1984.

Culbert, Samuel A., and John J. McDonough. *Radical Management: Power-Politics and the Pursuit of Trust*. New York: The Free Press, 1985.

Danforth, Douglas D. "The Quality Imperative." *Quality Progress* (February 1987): 17–19.

Davis, T. R., and R. Luthans. "Leadership Examined: A Behavioral Approach." *Academy of Management Review* 4 (1979): 237–48.

Deming, W. Edwards. *Out of the Crisis*. Cambridge, MA: Massachusetts Institute of Technology, Center for Advanced Engineering Study, 1986.

Depree, Max. *Leadership Is an Art*. New York: Doubleday, 1989.

Eadie, Douglas C. "Putting a Powerful Tool to Practical Use: The Application of Strategic Planning to the Public Sector." *Public Administration Review* 43 (September–October 1983): 447–52.

Erteszek, Jan J. "The Common Venture Enterprise : A Western Answer to the Japanese Art of Management?" *New Management* 1, no. 2 (1983): 4–10.

Etzioni, Amatai. *The Spirit of Community: Rights, Responsibilities and the Communitarian Agenda*. New York: Crown Publishers, 1993.

Evens, M. G. "Leadership Motivation." *Academy of Management Journal* 13 (1970): 91–102.

Fairholm, Gilbert W. *Values Leadership: Toward a New Philosophy of Leadership*. Westport, CT: Praeger, 1991.

———. *Organizational Power Politics: The Tactics of Leadership Power*. Westport, CT: Praeger, 1993.

———. "Leadership: A Function of Interactive Trust." *Journal of Leadership Studies*, 2, no. 2 (1994a): 9–19.

———. "Leading Diverse Followers," *Journal of Leadership Studies*, 1, no. 4 (1994b): 82–93.

———. *Capturing the Heart of Leadership: Spirituality and Community in the New American Workplace*. Westport, CT: Praeger, 1997.

Fayol, Henri. *General and Industrial Management*. [1906] New York and London: Pitman, 1949.

Floun, E. L. "Look and Listen: A Personal Primer on Leadership." *Vital Speeches of the Day* 153, no. 19 (July 15, 1987): 594–96.

Gardner, John W. *Self-Renewal: The Individual and The Innovative Society*. New York: Harper Colophon Books, 1964.

———. "Leadership and the Future." *The Futurist*, 24, no. 3 (1990): 8–12.

George, Claude S., Jr. *The History of Management Thought*. Englewood Cliffs, NJ: Prentice-Hall. 1968.

Gibb, Jack R. *A New View of Reason and Organization Development*. New York: The Guild of Tutors Press, 1978.

Gitlow, Howard, and Shelly Gitlow. *The Deming Guide to Achieving Quality and Competitive Position*. New York: Prentice-Hall, 1987.

Good, O. "Individuals, Interpersonal Relations and Trust." In Diego Gambetta, ed., *Trust: Making and Breaking Cooperative Relations*. Cambridge, MA: Basil Blackwell, 1988.

Goss, Tracy, Richard Pascale, and Anthony Athos. Quoted in *The New Leders*, John Renesch, ed. San Francisco: Sterling and Stone, March–April, 1994.

Graham, John. "Prescription for Success Overlooks Today's Harsh Realities." *Business Realities* (January 1994).

Graves, Clare W. "Toward Humanism from Animalism, An Open Systems Theory of Values." *Journal of Humanistic Psychology* (October 1970).

Greenleaf, Robert K. *Servant Leadership: A Journey into the Nature of Legitimate Power and Greatness*. New York: Paulist Press, 1977.

Grifin, Gerald R. *Machiavelli on Management*. New York: Praeger, 1991.

Gulick, L. M., and L. Urwick, eds. *Papers on the Science of Administration*. New York: Institute of Public Administration, Columbia University Press, 1937.

Handy, Charles. *The Age of Paradox*. Cambridge, MA: Harvard University Press, 1994.

Haney, William V. *Communication and Organizational Behavior*. Homewood, IL: Richard D. Irwin, Inc., 1973.

Bibliography

Harman, Willis. Quoted in John Renesch, ed., *New Traditions in Business: Spirit and Leadership in the 21st Century*. San Francisco: Berrett-Koehler, 1992.

Hart, Vivien. *Distrust and Democracy: Political Distrust in Britian and America*. New York: Cambridge University Press, 1978.

The Hartwick Humanities in Management Institute. "Jesus and the Gospels." *Hartwick Classic Leadership Cases*. Oneonta, NY: The Hartwick Humanities in Management Institute, 1993.

———. "Mahatma Gandhi." *Hartwick Classic Leadership Cases*. Oneonta, NY: The Hartwick Humanities in Management Institute, 1993a.

Hawley, Jack. *Reawakening the Spirit in Work: The Power of Dharmic Management*. San Francisco: Berrett-Koehler, 1993.

Heerman, Berry. "Spiritual Core is Essential to High Performing Teams." In *The New Leaders*, John Renesch, ed. San Francisco: Sterling and Stone, March–April, 1995.

Hickman, C. R. "Soul of Leadership." *Executive Excellence* 6, no. 12 (December 1989): 15–16.

Hitt, William D. *The Leader Manager: Guidelines for Action*. New York: Battelle Press, 1988.

Homans, G. C. *The Human Group*. New York: Harcourt Brace, 1956.

Honderich, T., and M. Burnyeat, eds. *Philosophy As It Is*. London: Penguin Books, 1979.

Jacobs, Devi. Quoted in *The New Leders*, John Renesch, ed. San Francisco: Sterling and Stone, November–December, 1994.

Jacobson, Stephen. "Spirituality and Transformational Leadership in Secular Settings: A Delphi Study." Ph.D. diss., Goleta College, 1995.

Jernigan, J. M. "Trust-Based Values Leadership: A Case Study in Productivity of a Public sector Line Organization." Ph.D. Diss., Virginia Commonwealth University, 1997.

Juran, Joseph M. *Juran on Leadership for Quality: An Executive Handbook*. New York: The Free Press, 1989.

Kantrowitz, Barbara. "In Search of the Sacred." *Newsweek*, November 28, 1994: 53–55.

Katz, D., and R. L. Kahn. *The Social Psychology of Organizations*. New York: John Wiley, 1966.

Keifer, Charles F. "Creating Metanoic Organizations." In John Renesch, ed., *New Traditions in Business: Spirit and Leadership in the 21st Century*. San Francisco: Berrett-Koehler, 1992.

Kostenbaum, Peter. *Leadership, the Inner Side of Greatness*. San Francisco: Jossey-Bass, 1991.

Kotter, John P. *Force for Change: How Leadership Differs from Management*. New York: The Free Press, 1990.

Kouzes, James M. and Barry Z. Posner. *The Leadership Challenge: How to Get Extraordinary Things Done in Organizations*. San Francisco: Jossey-Bass, 1987.

———. "Ethical Leaders." *Journal of Business Ethics* 11, no. 5–6 (May 1992): 479–484.

———. *Credibility: How Leaders Gain and Lose It, Why People Demand It*. San Francisco: Jossey-Bass, 1993.

Kuritz, Stephen J. "A Holistic Approach to Process Safety." *Occupational Health & Safety* 61, no. 10 (Oct 1992): 28–32.

Lammermeyr, Horst U. *Human Relations: The Key to Quality*. New York: ASQC Quality Press, 1990.

Lasswell, Harold D., and A. Kaplin. *Power and Society*. New Haven, CT: Yale University Press, 1950.

Levinson, Harry. *The Exceptional Executive: A Psychological Conception*. Cambridge, MA: Harvard University Press, 1968.

Lickert, R. *New Patterns of Management*. New York: McGraw-Hill, 1961.

Lorsch, Jay W. "Managing Culture: The Invisible Barrier to Strategic Change." *California Management Review* 28, no. 2 (Winter 1986).

Ludeman, Kate. *The Worth Ethic*. New York: E. P. Dutton, 1989.

Maccoby, Michael. *The Gamesman*. New York: Simon and Schuster, 1976.

———. *The Leader*. New York: Simon and Schuster, 1981.

McDermott, Linda C. "Keeping the Winning Edge: Strategies for Being a Business Partner." *Training and Development Journal* 41, no. 7 (July 1987): 16–19.

McGregor, Douglas. *The Human Side of Enterprise*. New York: McGraw-Hill, 1960.

McMillen, Kim. Quoted in *The New Leders*, John Renesch, ed. San Francisco: Sterling and Stone, September–October, 1994.

Magaziner, Elmer. "New Thinking, Not Just New Insight." In *The New Leaders*, John Renesch, ed. San Francisco: Sterling and Stone, January–February, 1994: 6.

Marquardt, Michael, and Angus Reynolds. *The Global Learning Organization*. New York: Irwin, 1994.

Martin, Merta M. "Leadership in a Cultural Trust Chasm: An Analysis of Trust Directed Behaviors and Vision Directed Behaviors That Lead to Positive Follower Attitude Responses." Ph. D. diss., Virginia Commonwealth University, 1996.

Mayo, Elton. *The Human Problems of an Industrial Civilization*. New York: Macmillan, 1933.

Merget, A. E. "Schools of Government Produce Too Many Managers, Too Few Leaders." *Governing* (November 1989): 90.

Mintzberg, Henry. *The Nature of Managerial Work*. New York: Harper & Row, 1973.

Mitroff, Ian I., Richard O. Mason and Christine M. Pearson. "Radical Surgery: What Will Tomorrow's Organizations Look Like?" *Academy of Management Executive* 8, no. 2 (May 1994): 11–21.

Myers, Ken. "A Culture of Value-added Leadership." *Executive Excellence* 10, no. 2 (February 1993): 4.

Myers, Scott. *Every Employee a Manager*. New York: McGraw-Hill, 1970.

Nadler, D. A., and L. Tushman. *Strategic Organization Design*. Glenview, IL: Scott Foresman, 1988.

Nair, Keshavan. *A Higher Standard of Leadership: Lessons from the Life of Gandhi*. San Francisco: Berrett-Koehler, 1994.

Naisbitt, J. *Megatrends: Ten New Directions Transforming Our Lives*. New York: Warner Books, 1982.

Naisbitt, John, and Aburdene, Patricia. *Reinventing the Corporation*. New York: Warner Books, 1985.

Odom, Randall Y., W. Randy Boxx, and Mark G. Dunn. "Organizational Cultures, Commitment, Satisfaction, and Cohesion." *Public Productivity & Management Review* XIV, no. 2 (1990): 157–69.

Ott, J. Steven. *The Organizational Culture Perspective*. Belmont, CA: The Dorsey Press, 1989.

Ouchi, William G. *Theory Z: How American Business Can Meet the Japanese Challenge*. New York: Avon Books, 1982.

Pascale, R. T., and Anthony G. Athos. *The Art of Japanese Management: Applications for American Executives*. New York: Simon and Schuster, 1981.

Pascerella, Perry. *The New Achievers: Creating a Modern Work Ethic*. New York: The Free Press, 1984.

Peters, Thomas J., and Nancy K. Austin. *A Passion for Excellence: The Leadership Difference*. New York: Random House, 1985.

Peters, Thomas J., and Robert H. Waterman, Jr. *In Search of Excellence*. New York: Harper and Row, 1982.

Peters, Tom. *Thriving on Chaos: Handbook for a Management Revolution*. New York: Knopf, 1987.

———. "Questions and Comments to Tom." *On Achieving Excellence* 9, no. 7 (July 1994): 9–11.

Pfeffer, Jeffrey. "The Ambiguity of Leadership." *Academy of Management Review* 2 (1977): 104–12.

———. *Power in Organizations*. Marshfield, MA: Pittman Publishing Co., 1981.

Pinchot, Gifford, and Elizabeth Pinchot. *The End of Bureaucracy and the Rise of the Intelligent Organization*. San Francisco: Berrett-Koehler, 1994.

Porter, E. A., A. G. Sargent and R. J. Stupack. "Managing for Excellence in the Federal Government." *New Management* 4, no. 4: 15–18.

Range, Peter Ross. "Interview with William J. Bennett." *Modern Maturity*, (March–April 1995).

Raspberry, William. "Churches Shouldn't Neglect their Strong Inside Game." *The Richmond Times-Dispatch*, Thursday, February 16, 1995: A15.

Reuss, L. E. "Catalysts of Genius, Dealers in Hope." *Vital Speeches of the Day* 53, no. 6 (January 1, 1987): 173–76.

Reynolds, Joe. "Boards of Directors as Corporate Stewards." *Directorship* (July–August 1994): 8–12.

Reynolds, P. D. "Organizational Culture as Related to Industry, Position, and Performance: A Preliminary Report." *Journal of Management Studies* 23, no. 3 (1986): 334–45.

Rosen, Robert H. "Developing a Healthy Organization." In John Renesch, ed., *New Traditions in Business: Spirit and Leadership in the 21st Century*. San Francisco: Berrett-Koehler, 1992.

Rossiter, Charles M., Jr., and Barnett W. Pearch. *Communicating Personally*. New York: Bobbs-Merrill Co., 1975.

Rowan, Roy. *The Intuitive Manager*. Boston: Little Brown, 1986.

Rupert, P. "Compelling Strategies for a Competitive Workplace." *Equifax* (1991): 15.

Samuelson, R. J. "In Search of Simplicity." *Newsweek*, April 30, 1984: 70.

Sathe, Vijay. "Organizational Culture: Some Conceptual Distinctions and Their

Managerial Implications." Working Paper, Harvard Business School, Division of Research, July 1983.

Schein, Edgar H. *Organizational Culture and Leadership*. San Francisco: Jossey-Bass, 1985.

Scott, W. G., and D. K. Hart. *Organizational America*. Boston: Houghton Mifflin, 1979.

Selznick, P. *Leadership in Administration*. Evanston, IL: Row, Peterson, 1957.

Senge, Peter. "The Leaders' New Work: Building Learning Organizations." *Sloan Management Review* (Fall 1990).

Senge, Peter, Charlotte Roberts, Richard Ross, Bryan Smith and Art Kleiner. *The Fifth Discipline Fieldbook: Strategies and Tools for Building a Learning Organization*. New York: Currency/Doubleday, 1994.

Steers, R. M. "Antecedents and Outcomes of Organizational Commitment." Ph.D. diss., University of Iowa, 1985.

Stogdill, R. M. *Leadership and Structures of Personal Interaction*. Columbus, OH: State University, Bureau of Business Research, 1957.

Tannenbaum, Robert, and Warren H. Schmidt. "How To Choose a Leadership Style." *Harvard Business Review* 51 (May–June 1973): 162–72.

Taylor, F. W. *The Principles of Scientific Management*. New York: W. W. Norton & Company, 1911.

Terry, Robert W. "Authentic Leadership: Courage in Action." *The New Leaders* (January–February 1994): 10.

Thayer, F. C. "Values, Truth and Administration: God or Mammon." *Public Administration Review* (January–February, 1980): 91–98.

Thompson, D. F., "The Possibility of Administrative Ethics," *Public Administration Review*, 45 (September–October 1985): 555–61.

Uttal, B. "The Corporate Culture Vultures," *Fortune* 108, no. 8 (1983): 66.

Vaill, Peter B. *Managing As a Performing Art: New Idea for a World of Chaotic Change*. San Francisco: Jossey-Bass, 1989.

Vroom, Victor H., and Philip W. Yetton. *Leadership and Decision-Making*. Pittsburgh: University of Pittsburgh Press, 1973.

Waterman, Robert. Quoted in *The New Leaders*, John Renesch, ed. San Francisco: Sterling and Stone, September–October 1994.

Wheatley, Margaret, J. *Leadership and the New Science: Learning About Organization from an Orderly Universe*. San Francisco: Berrett-Koehler, 1993.

Wildavsky, Aaron. *The Nursing Father: Moses As a Political Leader*. Birmingham: University of Alabama Press, 1984.

Yukl, Gary A. *Leadership in Organizations*. Englewood Cliffs, NJ: Prentice-Hall, 1981.

Zaleznick, A. "Managers and Leaders: Are They Different?" *Harvard Business Review* 29 (May–June 1977): 67.

Zand, D. E. "Trust and Managerial Poblem Solving." *Administrative Science Quarterly* 17 (1972): 229–39.

Index

accountability, 15, 107, 148
active listening, 96
ambition, 124
applying spiritual leadership, 143–54;
 building community, 149; other
 spiritual leadership techniques,
 153–54; setting a higher moral
 standard, 143; stewardship, 146
attitudes, 89
authority, 9

Barker, Joel, xvi, xvii
Barnard, Chester, 152
behavior, 11
behavioral theory, 52
belief systems, 121, 135–36
building shared values, 144
building trust, 93. *See also* trust development
business, 27; current situation, 123–
 28, 137; practice of, 132

career, 123
caring, 42, 83, 129
celebrating successes, 154
celebrations, 34

change, 19, 75; external forces, 75;
 shaping of, 89–90
change management, 52
chaos, 112
coaching, 43
cohesiveness, 83
comfort, 120
commitment, 82–83
communication, 82, 88; meaning, 107;
 spiritual, 129
community, 140, 150; building, 140;
 and personal wholeness, 140–41;
 spiritual 153
compartmentalize, 122
conflict, 82
contingency theory, 53
control, 11, 15, 82
cooperation, 82
coordination, 17
counciling-with, 64
courtesy, 41
Covey, Stephen B., 131, 135
cultural change, xvi
cultural factionalism, 10
cultural relativism, 104
cultural unity, 75–80, 106, 151

cultural values, 59, 78–79
culture: American, 76–77; creation of, 63, 78; definition of, 81–85; development of, 82–83, 96–97, 102; elements of definition, 83–85; leadership of, 77–78; meaning in, 90; trust, 78
culture setting, 45; attitudes, 89; change, 87–90; communications, 88; effectiveness levels, 89; office politics, 89; organizational action, 89; strategic planning, 88; techniques, 87–88

deciding, 11
definition of leadership, ix, x, xiii
Deming, W. Edwards, 25, 31–32, 36–37
demographics, 126
directing, 11
diversity, 105–8

effectiveness, 89
empowerment, 44, 97–98
enabling, 145, 154
ethics, 21–22
excellent leadership, 23–54
exchange theory, 52
expectations, 52, 93

Fairholm, Gilbert W., xxiii, 39, 85, 112, 132
Fayol, Henri, 3, 9
feeling, 121
focusing, 42, 96
force of spirit, the, 129–30
fostering the intelligent organization, 154
fragmented cultures, 107
freedom, 152

global facilitation, 154
Graves, Clare W., xvii
Great Man theory, 50
Greenleaf, Robert K., xi
Gulick, Luther, 3

happiness, 16, 71, 120
harmonious trust cultures, 76

harmony, 117
Hawthorne studies, 12
headship, xiii, 6, 50, 58
healthy organizations, 153
helping, 68
helping relationship, 95–96
high moral standards, 129, 132, 141; building shared values, 144; common ethical values, 146; enabling, 145; influence and power, 145; integrity, 144; service, 146; setting of, 143–46; sharing meaning, 145; transformation, 145; vision setting, 144
high quality, 26, 40
historical trends, 26
holistic leadership, 122, 135–36
humanistic theory, 53

influence, 145
inner certainty, 120
innovation, 29–30, 99
inspiration, 98–99
integration of spirituality into secular work organizations, 118, 131–32, 135–36
integrity, 144
intuition, 145

Jacobson, Stephen, 112, 117
Japanese models, 25
job rotation, 21
Juran, Joseph M., 31, 37
justice, 70

knowledge work, xiv

leader, as teacher, 64, 65
leader action technologies, 40–43; caring behavior, 42; common courtesy, 41; management by wandering around, 41–42; paying attention, 42–43; personal, 40–43
leader action technologies, to change the organization: culture setting, 45; standard setting, 45; strategic planning, 45; vision setting, 45–46

leader action technologies, toward stakeholders: coaching, 43–44; empowerment, 44

leadership, ix, xiii, 114; coaching, 43; as excellent management, xx, 25; goals of, 114; history, 2–4, 5–6, 26–27; importance of, xiii; levels of, xviii–xix; as management, xx, 3, 5, 17; mind-set, xiv, xv, 112, 118; results, 85; and spirit, 112; style, 96; technologies, 33; and trust, 91; in trust cultures, 78

leadership, alternative ways to think about, xv; culture change, xvi; paradigms, xvi–xvii; states of being, xvii–xviii

leadership as management, xx, 3, 5, 17 ; as excellent (good) management, xx, 25; trust culture leadership, xxii; spiritual (whole-soul) leadership, xxii; values-based leadership, xxi

leadership excellence, 25–46; functions, 18–22; history, 26–27; principles, 28–30; quality focus, 27–28; skills, 39–46, 153

leadership functions, 18–22; changes, 19; ethics, 21–22; motivation, 21; objectives, 19; participation, 21; performance appraisal, 20; reassignment and job rotation, 21; total quality focus, 19–20; trust, 19

leadership of trust cultures, 96–100; empowerment, 97–98; innovation, 99–100; inspiration, 98–99; ownership, 100; quality, 99; team building, 97

leadership skills, xiii, 39–46, 54; organizational, 44–46; personal, 40–43; to stakeholders, 43–44; team building, 103, 153

leadership theory, 49–50, 123, 137; shortcomings, 54; what the leader does, 51–53; where the leader does it, 53; who the leader is, 50–51

leadership versus management, 54–56

leading diverse workers, 103–5

liberty, 70

life force, 117

life purposes, 121

listening, 96

management, 3–4; functions, 18–22; purposes, 17

management by wandering around, 41

meaning, 107, 121; sharing of, 145

Mintzberg, Henry, xiv, 4, 12–13

moral leadership, 132

motivation, 21

Newtonian model, 123

objectives, 10, 19

obstacles to shaping trust cultures, 108

office politics, 88

office romance, 108

operations research, 14

organizational action, 84

organizational culture, 81

organizational structure, 14–16, 153

organizational values, 57

organizing, 10

ownership, 100

paradigms, xvi–xvii, xviii

participation, 21

paying attention, 42, 96

performance appraisals, 20

personal awareness, 117

personal transformation, 118, 132, 146

Peters, Tom, and Nancy K. Austin, 27

Peters, Tom, and Robert Waterman, 27, 41, 59

Pinchot, Gifford, and Elizabeth Pinchot, 15, 18, 152

planning, 10

POSDCORB, 8, 12

power use, 6, 127–28, 145

practical (work) spirituality, 111, 114, 131–33

principle-centered leadership, 135

principles of leadership excellence, 28–30; values-based leadership, 61–65

productivity, ix, 30, 59, 70–71

professionalism and spirit, 124

psychological theories, 51

quality, 26, 99; definition, 31–35; focus on, 28; history, 31–32; methods, 33–35; total quality management (TQM), 32, 33, 35–36

Quality Circles, 26, 27, 32, 34

Quantitative Management, 13

reassignment, 21

relationships, 63; individual, 63–64

religion, 113, 117, 119, 130, 132

respect for life, 70

rewards, 129

risk taking, 61, 145

role of leadership historically, 57–58

sameness amid diversity, 104–5

Scientific Management movement, 7–8, 12, 26–27

self-interest, 114, 120, 124, 125, 134

self-trust, 94

Selznick, Phillip, 54

Senge, Peter, xi, 113, 132

servant leadership, xi

servanthood, 118, 140, 146

service, 29, 146, 149

shaping culture, 87–90; techniques, 87–88

shaping service goals, 118

shared governance, 100

shared values, 76

situational theory, 53

social change, 75

social subsystems, 127

soul, xxiii, 131–32, 137

sources of support, 120

spirit, 111; power of, 127–28

spiritual leadership, xxiii, 112; definition of, 113, 115–22; elements of, 138; foundations of, 118–19; need, 118; setting a higher moral standard, 129, 132; shift to, 132; significance of, 132; the soul of, 131–32; a spiritual focus, 113; theory, 133, 137–41; visioning, characteristics of, 116, 132; in work life, 111

spiritual leadership model, 118, 138–41; goal, 141; process, 140–41; tasks, 139–40

spiritual leadership problems, 124–25; and ambition, 124; and energy, 136–37; and professionalism, 124; and self-overcoming, 125

spiritual values, 115, 116, 117, 154

spiritual wholeness, 116, 140–41. See also wholeness

spirituality: and leadership, 129–30; and moral rightness, 129, 132, 154; and workplace, 113

spirituality in the workplace, 113–15, 154; demographics, 126; formal subsystems, 127; nature of the workplace, 126; pressure of spirit, 126; pressures 126–27; work contracts, 127

spirituality shift, 130, 133–35

spiritually renewing activities, 134–35

stakeholder development, 62

state of being, xvii

standards, 107, 130

standard setting, 25

steward-leadership, 149–50

stewardship, 141, 150; higher-level council, 148–50; team, 147; team structure, 148, 150; the team council, 150

strategic planning, 88

strength, 120

success, an old/new definition, 128, 130–31

systems theory, 13, 52

Tannenbaum, Robert, and Warren H. Schmidt, 51

Taylor, Frederick W., 5, 7

teaching, 64, 65

team building (development), 97

teams, 151; definition of, 95

total quality management (TQM), 19, 32–33, 35–36
trait theory, 50–51
transcendent life, 121
transformation, 118, 132, 146, 151
trust, 19, 83; building of, 94; constraints on, 108; in leadership, 92; mutual, 77; results of, 93–94
trust building, 93
trust culture, 78, 108
trust culture leadership, xxi–xxii
trust development, 78–79, 101; through active listening, 96; through a consistent leadership style, 96; through helping, 95–96; through participation, 95
trust relationships, 94
trust-truth model, 92–94
trust values, 97
trustworthiness, 94

understanding spirit at work, 134
unity, 70–71, 131, 151

values, x, 79–80, 153; American, 105; shaping, 87
values-based transformational leadership theory, 61–65, 118; culture

of, 69; model of, 67–71; principles of, 61–65; productivity, 71–72; results of, 71–72
values displacement, 85
values foundation of spiritual leadership, 132
values leadership, xxi, 55; definition of, 55–60; philosophy of, 56–57, 58; principles, of, 61–65; results of, 64–65; theory, 59–60
values supporting personal professional spirituality, 115
values theory, 60
virtual environments, 118, 123, 131
Virtual Reality, xv
vision, 118, 119; creating the, 62–63; focus on, 29
visioning, 69–70
vision setting, 45–46

wholeness, 122, 135–36
work, 126; contracts, 127; goals of, 118, 124, 130; power of, 113; spirit in, 111, 114, 150, 152; understanding of, 111; structure, 152
workforce diversity, 106

Zand, Dale E., 94

About the Author

GILBERT W. FAIRHOLM is Emeritus Professor, Graduate Program
at Virginia Commonwealth University, Adjunct Associate Professor of
Leadership at the University of Richmond, and Visiting Professor at
Hampden-Sydney College. In addition to his academic appointments,
he has over twenty years of management experience in state and local
government. His previous award winning books include *Capturing the
Heart of Leadership* (1997) and *Leadership and the Culture of Trust*
(1994) published by Praeger Publishers.

ISBN 1-56720-202-0

90000>

9 781567 202021

EAN

HARDCOVER BAR CODE